A[
640[
Albu[

D0546531

BODYBUILDING
BASICS

BODYBUILDING BASICS

Robert Kennedy

 Sterling Publishing Co., Inc. New York

Library of Congress Cataloging-in-Publication Data

Kennedy, Robert, 1938–
    Bodybuilding basics / Robert Kennedy.
      p.   cm.
    Rev. ed. of: Start bodybuilding. c1984.
    Includes index.
    ISBN 0-8069-7392-7
    1. Bodybuilding.   2. Bodybuilding for women.   I. Title.
  II. Title: Body building basics.
    GV546.5.K463   1991
    646.7'5—dc20   90-28701
                                       CIP

10 9 8 7 6

© 1991 by Robert Kennedy
Published by Sterling Publishing Company, Inc.
387 Park Avenue South, New York, N.Y. 10016
Distributed in Canada by Sterling Publishing
% Canadian Manda Group, P.O. Box 920, Station U
Toronto, Ontario, Canada, M8Z 5P9
Distributed in Great Britain and Europe by Cassell PLC
Villiers House, 41/47 Strand, London WC2N 5JE, England
Distributed in Australia by Capricorn Ltd.
P.O. Box 665, Lane Cove, NSW 2066
Manufactured in the United States of America
All rights reserved

Sterling ISBN 0-8069-7392-7

647.75
KEN

CONTENTS

Francois Muse of France.

1
THE FIRST STEPS

You know very little, perhaps nothing, about the world of bodybuilding. In a short time you will have mastered the basics—at least in your mind. In Chapter 7 we will cover the exact performance of your exercises detailing how each movement builds and shapes your muscles.

Medical Checkup

First things first: Before taking up a new activity, especially a strenuous one like bodybuilding, it is always wise to seek the approval of your family doctor. By all means show him this book so that he can see exactly what you are talking about. Chances are, of course, he will be delighted that you will be exercising regularly. In some cases, especially if you are over forty years of age or have a history of ill health, he may arrange for you to take a simple stress test as a means of assessing your current health and tolerance levels for strenuous physical exercise. Should you have any inherited or known health problems such as heart, circulatory or organic irregularities, then make sure your doctor is made aware of these conditions. Smokers and heavy drinkers are doubly at risk, and should always check with their physicians before adopting a new diet or physical regimen.

Bodybuilding Exercises

The essence of bodybuilding consists of the regular performance of "progressive resistance" exercises, which usually involve the use of free weights (barbells and dumbbells) and free weight machines (apparatus on which free weights are loaded).

The idea behind "progressive resistance" is that your exercises can be tailored to your age, condition and specific strength levels. You can start, for example, by bench pressing a weight of forty pounds, and then as your fitness and power levels increase, you can add weight to the bar in the form of weight discs. These usually come in 1¼, 2½, 5, 10, 15, 25, and 50 pound increments. Powerlifters even go so far as to use 100 pound discs.

The Safety Factor

Because progressive resistance movements are tailored to your strength levels, the sport of bodybuilding is potentially very safe. If you follow the basic rules of performance you can go for many years injury-free. Bear in mind that all sports, some more than others, open up the likelihood of injury. Injury is even more of a problem with those who push their accomplishment levels to the maximum. Witness the sports champions of the world whose peak performance leaves them vulnerable to injury at the slightest deviation from perfect form.

As stated above, bodybuilding is a relatively safe sport. We have no body contact as seen in hockey, soccer or football. There are no body slams as experienced in wrestling, karate and judo, and certainly no danger of falls or crashes as one might experience in a variety of sports including horse racing, mountain climbing, car racing, cycling, motor cross, or even tennis.

The following are some basic safety procedures to follow in your progressive resistance workouts. Make them part of your training and you should have an accident-free training career.

1. Always bench press with a partner to hand you the weight. Your partner should not let go of the barbell until you have secured control and said the word "Right" or "Okay." When handing off the weight to your training partner (at the conclusion of the exercise) always make sure that the bar is *away* from your face. In the unlikely event that your partner fails to hold the bar securely, it would not fall on the chest, neck, or head.

2. Never be tempted to "try your strength" on a lift which is considerably heavier than you've ever lifted before. A friend and I were jokingly reminiscing over our strength of days gone by. On the floor was a heavy dumbbell. Laughingly, I said, "Remember when we could press a dumbbell over our heads weighing 140 pounds. . . ." My friend strode over to the dumbbell with a sudden determination, and hoisted it to his shoulders. He jerked it up and down several times and replaced it on the floor. In his face was a look of pride. In his trapezius was a warmth and gentle tingling. The next

day he could hardly move. The exertion of hoisting and jerking the heavy dumbbell had caused a pinched nerve condition. Now, several years later, it causes constant pain and has resulted in loss of muscle mass from the shoulder to the triceps and forearm of the left arm.

3. Always use a training partner when squatting. Getting "caught" in the low position of a squat, unable to raise up with a heavy weight on your back, is a most harrowing experience. Without a training partner one has a single option . . . utter collapse. A back injury, or worse, can easily result.

4. All apparatus should be checked before use. Make sure that cables are not excessively worn, and that benches and other units are sturdy and reliable. Remember that when you are bench pressing a weight, that the bench has to be capable of withstanding the total of your bodyweight *plus* the weight of the loaded bar you are exercising with. This can be a formidable poundage.

Check that dumbbell and barbell collars are secure before lifting. A couple of 10-pound discs dropped on your head can be pretty uncomfortable.

5. Take care when walking around the gym. Some of the exercise units may have sharp corners and could cause severe bruising or even a cut. Never step on loose weight discs or try to balance on a barbell. Stubbed toes are the most common gym injury. Admittedly not life threatening, but definitely an unneeded discomfort. Watch your step.

6. When removing weights from bench press racks, squat bar, or other apparatus, make sure that you have a firm grip on the disc. Take care not to drop them. Concentrate on what you are doing. A 50-pound disc may slide off easily, but as it comes off the bar it turns into dead weight. If you don't have a tight grip, you could end up with a broken foot.

Sets and Reps

Your workout is made up of repetitions (reps) and sets. A rep is a single count of an exercise. In other words if you press a barbell up to arm's length once, that is known as one rep. Perform it twice and we have two reps, etc. When we perform a series of reps (the average is 10–12) and then put the weight down for a breather, this is known as a set. Three sets of 10 repetitions in bodybuilding language is written "3 × 10". An exercise is seldom performed more than two or three sets in the beginners' stages. Intermediates will settle on 3–5 sets per exercise, and advanced bodybuilders will perform 4–8 sets per exercise, sometimes even more.

Warming Up

We should always warm up our muscles before each exercise. In other words, when we begin an exercise, the first set should only be done with a moderate weight using high repetitions. Typically, if, for example, we normally bench press 150 pounds for 3 sets of 10 reps, we would warm up with about half that weight (75 pounds) for 15–20 reps. Warming up readies the muscles for the heavier weights, "oils up" the joints, stretches the tendons and generally reduces the likelihood of minor tears and strains.

In addition to warming up for each exercise, it makes sense to also warm up the entire circulatory system by starting our workout with a general nonapparatus exercise such as rope jumping, stationary bike riding, stair climbing, or running in place. This activity should be restricted to five or ten minutes and is advocated solely to get the blood circulating strongly so that the heart and lungs, and other organs, are prepared for future action.

Dinah Anderson.

2

YOUR FIRST WORKOUT

There are two ways to get started in bodybuilding. You can attend a gym or train at home. Both have advantages and disadvantages. Home training, of course, can be totally private, and you can learn how to perform the exercises from the descriptions in this book. On the other hand, you will need to pur-chase some basic apparatus. Absolutely essential would be a flat bench that has an incline option, a pair of squat stands with safety catchers and a set of free weights, including a 6-foot bar and a pair of dumbbell rods. If you are really se-rious about maximizing progress, you would also include a sturdy lat machine, a thigh extension–leg curl bench, a

Alyssa Ferrari and the scintillating Shawn Ray.

Clothing

What to wear? Choose loose, comfortable clothing. Wear a sweat suit, exercise outfit, or shorts and tank. Take a look at body conditioning magazines like *MuscleMag International*, *Iron Man*, *Flex*, or *Shape* to see what people are wearing in the gym. The important aspect to consider is that your clothing never interferes with exercise performance or comfort. Some bodybuilders start their workouts wearing several sweat tops and then as the workout progresses, and they get hotter, layers are shed, one top at a time.

Warm Up

Once on the gym floor, you are ready to go. Start with a simple warm up. Perhaps the easiest thing to do is to ride a stationary bike for 10 minutes. Pedal at a brisk, even pace with the tension control set at moderate. This is not the time to either test your strength or to go for a speed record. You are simply warming up the heart and getting the blood coursing through the body at a faster rate. Should you not have access to a stationary bike, then warm up by running in place or by jumping rope.

The Exercises

Your first routine. Perform each exercise one set of 12–15 reps using a very light weight. Never start bodybuilding with poundages that overstress the muscles and make a movement difficult to perform. Naturally, readers of this book will vary in age and strength levels, so I cannot recommend any starting poundage that would be ideal for all. However, I have made some broad proposals. Use more or less than my suggested starting poundages based on how you feel they apply to your own levels of physical condition. Here are the exercises for your first training session. Their exact performance is described in detail in Chapter 7.

preacher curl unit, a hack slide machine, and a standing calf raise apparatus.

A gym membership, of course, will get you all of the above and more, but annual fees can be burdensome; certainly, building your own home gym will save you money in the long run. Bear in mind though, there is more competition at a commercial gym, and you'll make better progress training in the vicinity of others. Training at home, however, can be done at any time and you won't have to fight heavy traffic or adverse weather conditions travelling to and from commercial establishments after a hard day at the office.

Press Behind Neck (shoulders)
12 repetitions.
Starting poundage (men)   40 pounds
Starting poundage (women) 20 pounds

Bench Press (chest)
12 repetitions
Starting poundage (men)   60 pounds
Starting poundage (women) 30 pounds

Regular Squat (upper legs) 15 repetitions
Starting poundage (men)   75 pounds
Starting poundage (women) 40 pounds

Bent Over Rowing (upper back)
15 repetitions
Starting poundage (men)   60 pounds
Starting poundage (women) 30 pounds

Prone Hyper-Extension (lower back)
15 repetitions
Starting poundage (men)   none
Starting poundage (women) none

Standing Calf Raise (lower legs)
15 repetitions
Starting poundage (men)   50 pounds
Starting poundage (women) 30 pounds

Lying Triceps Curl (back of upper arms)
12 repetitions
Starting poundage (men)   30 pounds
Starting poundage (women) 15 pounds

Barbell Curl (top of upper arm)
12 repetitions
Starting poundage (men)   40 pounds
Starting poundage (women) 20 pounds

Wrist Curl (forearms) 15 repetitions
Starting poundage (men)   40 pounds
Starting poundage (women) 20 pounds

Lying Leg Raise (abdominals)
15 repetitions
Starting poundage (men)   none
Starting poundage (women) none

Exercise Performance

Beginners should perform all exercises in perfect style; that is to say, you should lift a weight slowly under complete control (aim for a 2 seconds up and 2 seconds down time span).

Never bounce a bench press weight on your chest (it could crack your sternum). Avoid bouncing in the squat exercise (damaged knees could result). Stay clear of excessive leaning back in overhead press or exaggerated arching while flat or incline benching dumbbells or barbells. Keep your back flat while squatting, dead lifting, rowing or cleaning a weight.

In exercises like wide-grip pulldowns and chins, keep the elbows back throughout the movement. Don't lean back excessively while curling. It is a good practice to avoid any type of ballistic movement when training with resistance exercise. Make the muscles do the lifting rather than relying on momentum to get the weight from A to B.

As a beginner, strict exercise style (otherwise known as perfect form) is required. You have to learn control in the beginning stages. Admittedly, as you progress and become more experienced in the world of Iron, rules can be broken. In some cases, the strict style of training can be done away with and substituted with "cheating" methods. But again, your right to cheat must be earned by your apprenticeship of adhering to the initial principles of perfect form for at least a 6-month period (see chapter on training systems). For now, keep it strict.

Britain's Bertil Fox displays his awesome mass while performing the concentration curl.

3

PRINCIPLES TO TRAIN BY

Questions, questions, questions. You have a million of them. That's why you're reading this book. Certainly, a question can, and often does, have a variety of answers. It could even be argued that there are as many different answers as there are questions. How do you know that the advice I give you is the correct advice? You don't. All I can do is promise you that it is the best and most honest advice I can find in me.

My experience in bodybuilding is rare if not completely unequalled. It's no exaggeration to say that less than a handful of people on this earth have my first-hand knowledge of the sport experience that incorporates being a practicing bodybuilder (having competed in powerlifting, weightlifting and physique competitions). Unlike the big names in bodybuilding, I actually write every word of the books that carry my name as exclusive author. Additionally, I have attended more top contests from a variety of organizations (Wabba, AAU, IFBB, Nabba, NPC, etc.) than any other human being, plus I have the inside lane on the thinking and training patterns of literally hundreds of famous Iron Game personalities, developed through the publication and editorship of my own magazine *MuscleMag International*.

I have an endless "day long" communication, via telephone, fax, and correspondence with the stars of our sport. Everyone who is anyone has shared his or her thoughts on the disciplines of bodybuilding for the readers of *Muscle-Mag International*.

Blowing my own horn is not natural to me. I do it not to inflate my own importance, but merely as an effort to put your mind at ease with regard to my competence to give out sound advice and workable instruction. Above all, I believe in my own words. I follow them, act upon them and live by them. Right now as I write this at 2:30 in the morning my house is quiet; only the purring of the refrigerator in the nearby kitchen is audible. Wife, child, and dogs are sleeping. . . . My entire thoughts are turned towards you, my reader. The following principles are my best shot at giving you the *most* workable advice and rules for the fastest production of muscle mass that I know of. There are no better methods than I'm giving you now—at least none that I'm aware of. My finger is on the pulse of bodybuilding from morning till night. No one is closer to the sport. No one is more sincere. The following principles will help you build big, shapely muscles in the fastest, safest way possible.

Frequency

How many times a week should you train? A natural trainer, and hopefully you are a natural trainer (i.e., you don't take anabolic steroids or other muscle enhancing drugs), should train each body part twice weekly. This is the ideal frequency for fast muscle growth. To train more frequently will likely cause you to eventually overtrain, especially if high intensity is used. This condition leaves you feeling drained, lacking in energy, but more importantly, all muscle enlargement will cease. Continual overtraining will even cause loss in size and strength. An additional "side effect" to overtraining is that the muscles may become flat or stringy looking.

Those who take steroids (and I am *strongly opposed to their use*) may be able to gain by training each body part three times a week but usually this is only for a 4–6 week period. Eventually the bodybuilder who trains in this manner will find that recuperation is not complete enough to allow for an acceptable rate of growth. Also, of course, there are many negatives involved with steroid taking, not least of which may be permanent damage to the vital organs.

There are dozens of accepted frequency methods. Here are the best ones.

Three times per week

As previously mentioned, training the whole body three times a week can be too much; however, it is sometimes a suitable method for the beginner, who usually trains with low intensity, low sets and with a short workout. The important point to observe when training the whole body three times a week is that you have a complete day's rest (no training) between workouts. Most people, therefore, train Mondays, Wednesdays and Fridays (to leave the weekend free), but you can also train on Tuesdays, Thursdays and Saturdays or any other combination that avoids training two days in a row.

Two on, one off

This is a great method for maximizing gains. Start by dividing your workout in two. This can be done in a variety of

Arnold Schwarzenegger always gave 100 percent.

ways. You could exercise your legs and back and biceps on day one, and train your chest, shoulders and arms on day two. Abdominals could be trained every workout day to ensure a tight waistline. This "two on, one off" system does not fit into the seven-day week routine, so you will find yourself taking your workouts on different days.

Three on, one off

This is the champions' frequency. More aspiring competitive bodybuilders train using the "three on, one off" system than any other. That is not to say that beginners can't benefit from this frequency system.

Start by dividing your routine into three parts. Arnold Schwarzenegger used to split his routine as follows when using this method:

> *Day one:* chest, biceps, forearms
> *Day two:* legs, triceps, lower back
> *Day three:* upper back, shoulders, abdominals

Of course, this system of three-way splitting is not carved in stone. But at the same time it didn't do too bad for the Austrian-born Schwarzenegger.

Every other day split

Everyone can gain from this frequency plan. It allows for maximum recuperation because each body part is trained slightly less than twice weekly. It's been an accepted system of training for thirty years, but it was "Mr. Heavy Duty" Mike Mentzer who popularized it, and made the bodybuilding public aware of its

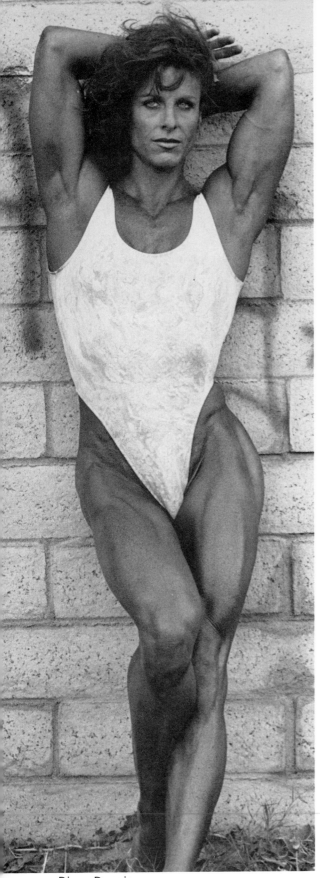

Diana Dennis.

workability. Here's how it works. Split your routine into two roughly equal segments. Perform the first half of your workout on day one. The following day is a rest day. No training. The next day you train on the second half of your routine. The day after that is a rest day again. In other words, you never train two days in a row. And, you never rest two days in a row. This method is especially useful to people whose recuperative powers are sluggish.

Intensity

Intensity is the amount of effort we put into our training. For the sake of argument we could refer to our workouts as low intensity, high intensity, or medium intensity. Low-intensity training is seldom very productive because the muscle isn't sufficiently challenged, but, of course, some toning does result as well as initial gains in muscle size.

High intensity is translated into a constant effort to add more weight, or get more reps. There is little doubt that by forcing the muscle to perform more work there is a corresponding increase in muscle size. However, there comes a time when trying to break new records in your workouts becomes self-defeating. We can't keep increasing reps and adding weight without burning out. And, constant high-intensity training leads to the fastest burnout of all. So, what's the answer? It is to cycle your training so that you train hard all the time, but not by using super-high intensity. You have to bring high-intensity training into your workout to reach for a new plateau, but once achieved this all-out effort must be reduced slightly, while at the same time holding onto the gains achieved from the extra push. Easier said than done, maybe, but it is the way to maintain progress. Let me repeat. You cannot employ high-intensity methods all the time, and expect progress. It just doesn't work.

Exercise Style

I believe that all beginners should work out using strict exercise form. That is to say, you should not swing the weight up, bounce it, jerk it, or otherwise employ momentum to raise the resistance. Use full-range movements with a slow deliberate style that involves no ballistic movement. A curl, for example, should start with the arms hanging straight down at the sides, elbows locked. Now, without any forward lean, knee bending or swinging, raise the barbell upward until the bar is at your throat. Lower under control and repeat. This is known as strict exercise form. The biceps do *all* the work. There is absolutely no assistance from the legs or back.

The same goes for all your exercises. Military style is the order of the day: No quick rebounds in the squat; no leaning back on your shoulder presses; no bouncing the bar on your chest in the bench press. Steve Reeves once remarked that a perfect physique can be built with perfect exercise style. Certainly, every beginning bodybuilder should train using strict form during the initiation period of bodybuilding. There comes a time, however, when some creative style changes can be utilized. But one has to train with perfect exercise form first. In time you will have earned the right to employ a looser style.

Regularity

Some call it stick-ability. Regular training as opposed to on-off training is one of the secrets of bodybuilding progress. It is not a fail-proof principle, however. There are thousands of regular trainers who never progress because they merely go through the actions of working out, but neglect to apply themselves positively.

On the other hand, you could practice the latest methods and apply the newest techniques, but without regular workouts you will be dooming yourself to failure.

Goal Setting

It could be said that nothing is achieved without planning. We have to have goals. It is the athlete who plans his campaign for physical excellence who eventually succeeds. Goal setting has to be done realistically. It is no good setting goals that are way beyond our reach. It is far better to set attainable goals within a realistic time frame. When they are achieved, then a new goal is set. This is the way to progress.

Rest Between Sets

Those who train purely for power should take longer rests between each set than those who exercise for muscle mass. Powerlifters and Olympic lifters frequently take 4 or 5 minutes rest between their sets, while a bodybuilder will typically take only 60–90 seconds, sometimes less. In fact, when supersetting (alternating 2 different exercises for 3 or 4 sets each), bodybuilders often allow themselves no more rest between sets than it takes to change exercises, a few seconds at most. As a general rule, you will get the most from your workouts if you allow only enough rest between sets to enable your breathing to normalize. It goes without saying that if you resume training *before* your breath has returned to normal then you are creating an increased oxygen debt.

This may be a fine way to challenge your heart and lungs, but the burden to the respiratory system will hinder your ability to exhaust the muscle. Your heart and lungs are overstressed before you can sufficiently stimulate the muscles. This can easily happen with "lung bursting" exercises like squats. Frequently, we have to quit the exercise because of a built-up oxygen debt, even though the quads haven't been fully exhausted.

Steve Stallard and Sheri Spivey of Miami Beach.

4

THE POWER FOODS

Can you imagine how many zillion words have been written about food. Good foods, bad foods, tasty foods, yucky foods? There are thousands of books on the subject, and almost everyone has a different approach. I like to use the term *moderation* when talking of nutrition. I believe in eating fresh, wholesome, healthy foods, but not to the extent that I could be labelled a health nut or food crank. The only time bodybuilders aim for 100 percent perfect nutrition each and every day without exception is during the last 6–8 weeks prior to an important contest. That's when they are near fanaticism and total dedication to the cause.

A bodybuilder cannot afford to eat foods that do not contribute to progress in a positive way. We have to eat well. We have to eat in a balanced way. You probably heard of the thousand and one junk foods that we refer to as "calorie-dense." Typical of these are potato chips, doughnuts, candies, regular breakfast cereals, sugars, and soft drinks. I call my list of power foods "nutrient dense"; that is to say, they contain a high percentage of vitamins and minerals per calorie. Others are particularly high in the kind of fibre that can lower cholesterol. Unlike Popeye who had the right idea (but needed more variety) you should make a habit of eating a large variety of foods. Popeye's spinach is a fine vegetable, a true power food, but there are plenty more where that came from: Here's my "all-time best" list of power foods to help you get 110 percent in body performance, health, strength and development.

Power Food #One: The Orange

Eat the whole orange, even some of the white pith. Do not substitute orange juice for a whole orange. There is a great difference between the two. Orange juice has little fibre and is absorbed too quickly. It has more concentrated sugar and less overall goodness. The plus value to a bodybuilder is the high vitamin C content (helps cement muscle cells and keep them strong) but the orange also contains high amounts of potassium and calcium.

Qualities per 5½-ounce orange

Protein	1.1 grams
Carbohydrates	13 grams
Fat	.16 gram
Vitamin A	270 I.U.
Vitamin B$_1$	.1 milligram
Vitamin C	67 milligrams
Calcium	52 milligrams
Potassium	235 milligrams
Magnesium	13 milligrams
Calories	58

Power Food #Two: Turkey

Together with other poultry meats, turkey contains substantial levels of tryptophan, an essential amino acid. Frank Zane was a great believer in supplementing with tryptophan, which he called his tranquility vitamin. It helped him sleep well after a heavy workout, and relieved him of nervous tension.

Four ounces of white meat poultry gives us about 27 grams of high class protein (amino acids), which is just about as much as anyone can assimilate at any one feeding.

Turkey and other poultry are low-fat meats, and consequently they make ideal bodybuilding foods. It is important to remember, however, that if you are using them as part of a low-fat diet, the skin is removed before eating. The white meat (breast) has less fat than the dark meat (legs and wings).

Qualities per 3 ounces of cooked turkey breast

Protein	20 grams
Carbohydrates	trace
Fat (unsaturated)	.30 gram
(saturated)	.69 gram
Vitamin B$_6$	.49 milligram
Vitamin B$_{12}$	.34 microgram
Niacin, a	
B vitamin	9.33 milligrams
Iron	.65 milligram
Potassium	210 milligrams
Phosphorus	164 milligrams
Calories	102

Power Food #Three: Milk

Milk has been called "the perfect food" because it contains almost every nutrient catalogued by man. In fact, nutritionists are pretty certain that milk contains all the micro nutrients that have yet to be discovered. Milk is our single best source of calcium. A cup of skim milk contains some 50 percent of a person's recommended daily allowance. Calcium can lower blood pressure and fortify bones. Bodybuilders have relied on milk for decades because nothing builds muscle mass as effectively.

Some people, especially some Asians, do not possess the enzymes that are needed to digest milk. This goes for many older people, too, who typically "lose" the enzymes as they mature. If you find that you can't digest milk (bloatedness) then try yogurt or the new acidophilus milks.

Qualities per 8-ounce glass of milk

Protein	8.3 grams
Carbohydrates	11.7 grams
Fat	1 gram
Vitamin A	500 I.U.
Vitamin B$_2$	.4 milligram
Vitamin D	100 I.U.
Calcium	295 milligrams
Magnesium	33 milligrams
Phosphorus	232 milligrams
Calories	104

Power Food #Four: Broccoli

High fibre and more densely packed with vitamins and minerals than almost any other food, broccoli is the king of vegetables.

Although broccoli is not considered a bodybuilding food in the sense of meat, fish, eggs or milk, it nevertheless delivers 4.7 grams of protein per cup; but the beauty of this vegetable is that it is extremely low in calories. It's very high in Vitamin C (essential for tissue repair) and Vitamin A (essential for liver and eye functions, plus it plays a key role in supplying the body's immune system with essential nutrients). Best way to cook it is to steam it, and remember to consume both the stems and the florets when eating broccoli.

Qualities per cup of broccoli (steamed)

Protein	4.7 grams
Carbohydrates	7 grams
Fat	.5 gram
Vitamin A	3800 I.U.
Niacin, a B vitamin	1.2 milligrams
Vitamin C	140 milligrams
Calcium	136 milligrams
Potassium	414 milligrams
Iron	1.2 milligrams
Calories	40

Power Food #Five: The Carrot

The list of good that may come from eating carrots, especially raw carrots, can make them seem almost like a miracle food. Carrots supply good amounts of Vitamin C and B and a comparatively large amount of Vitamin A. They also contain potassium and calcium, are high in complex carbohydrates and are a good source of fibre. Several studies have shown that eating just two carrots a day can reduce cholesterol levels by 10–20 percent.

Beta carotene, found in carrots, is an antioxidant that may defend the body against free radicals, harmful chemicals involved in cancer, heart disease and arthritis. Eaten raw, carrots act to clean the teeth and massage the gums as well as any toothbrush. They make an ideal snack for bodybuilders who wish to lower their bodyfat levels because they pack a heavy nutritional punch without the potentially fattening high calories associated with other high nutrition snacks.

Qualities per medium carrot

Protein	1 gram
Carbohydrates	5.0 grams
Fat	trace
Calcium	18 milligrams
Vitamin A	5500 I.U.
Calories	20

Power Food #Six: The Banana

Bananas are high in complex carbohydrates and are extremely high in potassium (directly connected to proper fluid balance and overall muscle tone), one of the body's most important elements found in each and every cell.

Bananas make an ideal snack for the bodybuilder. They deliver high quality nutrition when the body needs sustenance quickly.

Qualities per 6-ounce banana (weighed with skin)

Protein	1.18 grams
Carbohydrates	26.7 grams
Fat	.54 gram
Vitamin B$_6$	.64 gram
Biotin, a B vitamin	6 micrograms
Vitamin C	10 milligrams
Iron	.35 milligrams
Potassium	451 milligrams
Magnesium	33 milligrams
Calories	100

Power Food #Seven: The Potato

Old-fashioned diets invariably portrayed the potato as the food to avoid. It had a "bad guy" image. This was principally due to the fact that it delivers very high amounts of complex carbohydrates.

Traditionally, potatoes have been mutilated during the cooking procedure. They have been fried or roasted in fat, or eaten with loads of sour cream or butter, all of which served to catapult their calorie rating to enormous highs. Today most people still believe that potatoes are fattening. But on their own (baked), they deliver only a modest 82 calories per 4-ounce potato.

Potatoes supply loads of minerals and definitely have a place in a bodybuilder's diet.

Qualities per 4-ounce potato

Protein	2.12 grams
Carbohydrates	17.4 grams
Fat	.2 gram
Niacin, a B vitamin	1.5 milligrams
Vitamin C	16.5 milligrams
Magnesium	40 milligrams
Potassium	417 milligrams
Phosphorus	53 milligrams
Calories	82

Power Food #Eight: The Bean

Ask any World War Two veteran, or any cowboy. Beans are *it*.

Well, beans may not be the greatest delicacy in the world, but they sure are good for us. They provide a low-calorie source of protein, and thus join the ranks of making the bodybuilders' "dream-food" list. Beans are high in water-soluble fibre, the kind that can lower cholesterol levels pronto. Dried beans such as pinto, Great Northern, kidney, and navy supply B vitamins, iron, calcium, potassium and magnesium. Fresh green beans are also high in vitamins A and C.

Tofu is a soybean product enjoying growing popularity among Americans who follow the health, strength and fitness way of life. Beans can make a very nutritious between-meal snack, or can be combined with meats, fish or other vegetables to form a conventional "complete" meal.

Qualities of lima beans per cup (cooked)

Protein	2 grams
Carbohydrates	7 grams
Fat	trace
Vitamin A	680 I.U.
Vitamin C	15 milligrams
Calcium	63 milligrams
Calories	30

Power Food #Nine: Whole Grains

It can be argued that all grains are good for you, but whole grains (they contain the kernel with its germ and the bran) offer greatness to your nutritional program. Brown rice, for example, contains almost three times more fibre than unenriched white rice. It also contains three times more B vitamins, twice as much iron, three times more magnesium, 50 percent more zinc and a whopping five times more vitamin E.

Formerly known as the staff of life, whole wheat (bread) is perhaps the most nutritious grain of all. It contains the important B vitamins, which men tend to need more than women. Also contained in wheat are vitamin E, iron, potassium, magnesium and zinc, and its bran is one of the best sources of dietary fibre known. Most Americans eat between 5 and 14 grams of fibre a day, but many fitness experts recommend eating 20–35 grams daily to bring about optimum health and performance. Bodybuilders owe much of their basic development to the regular ingestion of whole grains. As a bonus factor, there is much evidence showing that whole grains can protect your heart by significantly lowering cholesterol.

Qualities per slice of whole-wheat bread

Protein	3 grams
Carbohydrates	15 grams
Fat	1 gram
Vitamin B_1	.06 gram
Vitamin B_2	.1 milligram
Niacin, a B vitamin	1 gram
Calcium	15 milligrams
Phosphorus	60 milligrams
Iron	0.7 gram
Calories	72

Power Food #Ten: Flat Fish

Sole, flounder, plaice and other flat fish, contain high amounts of a fatty acid known to improve general health by enhancing the state of the cardiovascular system and helping control the level of blood fats. The name of this fatty acid is eicosapentamoic acid (EPA).

Five ounces of steamed flat fish will deliver a full 25 grams of muscle-building protein, making it the perfect bodybuilding (cell-building) food. During the last few weeks prior to a contest, most successful bodybuilders include regular portions of flat fish in their diets.

Qualities per 4 ounces of steamed fillet

Protein	20 grams
Carbohydrates	0
Fat (unsaturated)	.63 gram
(saturated)	.31 gram
Vitamin B_{12}	1.3 micrograms
Niacin, a B vitamin	1.9 milligrams
Pantothenic acid, a B vitamin	.96 milligram
Phosphorus	220 milligrams
Iron	.9 milligram
Potassium	385 milligrams
Calories	92

* * *

Surprised at my top selection for a bodybuilder's menu? Did you expect me to list some exotic, secret foods?

It reminds me of the people who ask me about which exercises to use to build the various muscles. The last things they want to hear about are bench presses, rows, curls and dips. And certainly not squats! But these popular exercises are the most widely known because virtually every bodybuilder uses them. They work!

It's the same with foods. I would love to rattle off a list of little-known superfoods which all but guarantee to sprout muscles. It would have made this book an all-time best-seller in the world of bodybuilding. Can you imagine: "Robert Kennedy reveals his totally unique list of secret foods to build a fantastic body!" No, ordinary as my list may appear, these foods are really among the best known for providing the ultimate nutrition required by the aspiring bodybuilder. To me they are the Super Foods of the Universe. Now all you have to do is include them in your diet.

Base your diet on fresh natural foods, broiled meats, fish, whole grain cereals and bread, eggs, unsalted nuts, steamed vegetables, and salads.

Forget fried foods. Don't remove the peel from apples, tomatoes, peaches, and so on. Peel contains nutrients that the fruit itself does not. Wash fruit and vegetables, however, because insecticides can linger and cause intestinal problems.

To function perfectly, your body needs a combination of protein, carbohydrates, fats, vitamins, minerals, and water.

Protein

Known as the most essential of all, protein is required for building and repairing the body's cells—your muscles. It is essential even to those trying to lose weight, not just those who are trying to gain mass. During digestion, protein is broken.

Carbohydrates

Carbohydrates consist of sugars and starches. They are the body's main source of energy. (If your carbohydrates are low, your body may utilize protein for energy.) As you know, the body stores excess carbohydrates as fat.

Carbohydrate sources include potatoes, cereals, bread, cakes, spaghetti and other pasta, rice, bananas, lima beans, corn, dried fruits, honey, sugar, candy, and soft drinks.

Fats

Fats are used primarily as an energy source, but they are also instrumental in protecting the various internal organs. They help to regulate body temperature, and some supply large quantities of needed vitamins.

Fat sources are butter, margarine, cream, fatty meats, most cheeses, salad dressing, mayonnaise, egg yolks, nuts, fried foods, chocolate, rich desserts, peanut butter, and shortenings.

Minerals

The bones and teeth contain large amounts of the minerals calcium and potassium. However, other minerals are required to balance the body processes. Nerves, muscles, and organs require body fluids containing such minerals as sodium, potassium, and calcium.

The most important minerals are calcium (for teeth and bones), copper (for blood vessel normality), iodine (for energy regulation), iron (for prevention of anemia), magnesium (for building bones), phosphorus (for regulating metabolism), potassium (for healthy nerves and muscles), sodium (for absorption of glucose, and balancing the body acid base), and zinc (for normal growth and development).

Vitamins

Vitamins are needed so that food can be utilized and the body can function properly. Vitamins A, D, E, and K (fat soluble) are not needed daily and, in fact, too high a dosage can be harmful. However, the B vitamins and C (water soluble) are required daily. Excess is excreted in the urine. Deficiencies show up rapidly. Here are some of the vitamins and a few of their uses.

Vitamin A for healthy bones, skin, teeth, resistance to infection, and good vision. It is found in eggs, cheese, liver, tomatoes, butter, milk and milk products, and margarine.

Vitamin B₁ (thiamine) for a healthy nervous system. It is found in pork, organ meats such as liver, kidney, and heart, whole-grain breads, cereals, peas, nuts, beans, and eggs.

Vitamin B₂ (riboflavin) helps in the use of protein, fats, and carbohydrates for energy and tissue building. It promotes healthy skin, particularly around the mouth, nose and eyes. It is found in organ meats, liver, sausage, milk, cheese, eggs, whole-grain bread, dried beans, and leafy green vegetables.

Niacin promotes a healthy nervous system and skin, aids normal digestion, and helps cells use oxygen to release energy. It is found in liver, meats, fish, whole-grain breads, dried peas and beans, peanut butter, and nuts.

Vitamin B₆ (pyridoxine) aids in protein utilization and prevention of certain types of anemia. It is also helpful in maintaining normal growth. It is found in liver, kidneys, butter, meats, as well as in fish, cereal, soybeans, tomatoes, peanuts, and corn.

Pantothenic acid helps in the breakdown of fats, proteins, and carbohydrates for energy. It is found in organ meats, egg yolk, meats, fish, soybeans, peanuts, broccoli, cauliflower, potatoes, peas, cabbage, and whole-grain products.

Folic acid promotes the development of red blood cells, and the normal metabolism of carbohydrates, proteins, and fats. It is found in organ meats, asparagus, turnips, spinach, kale, broccoli, corn, cabbage, lettuce, potatoes, and nuts.

Vitamin B₁₂ produces red blood cells in bone marrow and builds new proteins. It helps the normal functioning of nervous tissue. It is found in liver, kidneys, lean meats, fish, hard cheese, and milk.

Vitamin C (ascorbic acid) helps "cement" cells together. It produces healthy teeth, gums, and blood vessels and improves iron absorption. It hastens the healing of wounds and resistance to infections. It also aids in the synthesis of hormones that regulate body functions. It is found in citrus fruits (grapefruit, oranges, lemons), strawberries, cantaloupes, raw vegetables (especially green peppers), cauliflower, broccoli, kale, tomatoes, potatoes, cabbage, and Brussels sprouts.

Vitamin D promotes healthy bones and teeth and helps the body absorb calcium and phosphorus. Found in liver, egg yolk, and foods fortified with vitamin D such as vitamin D milk, it is also produced in the body by exposure to direct sunlight.

Vitamin E protects red blood cells and retards destruction of vitamins A and C. It is found in wheat-germ oil, rice, leafy vegetables, nuts, margarine, and legumes.

Vitamin K permits blood clotting. It is found in spinach, kale, cabbage, cauliflower, and pork liver.

Weight Control

Normalizing your body weight is basically a matter of controlling your calorie intake. A calorie is a unit of heat energy. When a body takes in as many calories as it burns up, *thermodynamic balance* occurs. ("Thermo" means heat; "dynamic" refers to movement.)

One way of understanding thermodynamics is to think of it as a bank account. You begin with a given amount of money in the bank (fat on your body). Eating corresponds to making a deposit. Exercise (walking, running) can be likened to writing a check. If your deposits equal your withdrawals, your balance (weight) will stay the same. Burn more calories than you consume and your body will start losing weight. If

27

you wish to gain weight, increase your food intake considerably.

Many successful bodybuilders know the following basic rule: If you leave the table feeling "full to the brim" you will gain weight. If you leave the table "just satisfied" you will maintain bodyweight. If you leave the table "just a little hungry" you will lose weight.

A word of caution: Any diet should be balanced nutritionally. Simply choosing a menu of low- or high-calorie ingredients is not satisfactory. Never evaluate foods solely on their calorie count.

Generally, you should select foods from each of the following five main groups:

1. *Milk group* (milk, cheese, ice cream)

2. *Meat group* (beef, veal, lamb, pork, eggs, fish)

3. *Vegetable/Fruit group* (the fresher the better)

4. *Grain group* (bread, whole wheat)

5. *Fats group* (butter, margarine, oils; small amounts only)

Nutrition and the Athlete

Increased food intake, especially of high-protein foods, can be part of the muscle-building process. Body bulk can even be built from junk food, but if you are careless about quantities (overall calorie intake), then some of that muscle will be accompanied by fat. The two together, although different components entirely, are often referred to as *bulk.*

If an athlete wants to obtain only tendon power (added strength without large muscles), he should accompany his weight training with a high-protein, low-carbohydrate diet. In other words, his nutritional intake should be based on protein foods such as eggs, poultry, fish, hard cheese, meats, and skim milk.

He should eat a minimum of flour products, spaghetti, puddings, sugar, potatoes, rice, cakes, candies, and desserts, and avoid fried foods. The person who wants strength without extra body weight should obtain his vitamins and minerals from salads, tomatoes, spinach, zucchini, radishes, and citrus fruits.

The footballer, wrestler, or any other sportsman requiring additional weight should eat more of the "heavier" calorie foods. These include puddings, whole milk, potatoes, carrots, bananas, beans, strawberries and cream, gravies and thick wholesome soups, wholewheat bread, butter, and so on. (Some of these foods do, however, have a high cholesterol content.)

Muscle Does Not Turn to Fat

It is physiologically impossible for fat to turn into muscle or vice versa. It just cannot happen. Most bodybuilders, when they "lay off," or give up training permanently, lose weight. Because there is no regular demand (from their workouts) for large muscle size, it slowly diminishes. Practise at chess and your brain will become sharper. Take up running and you will get faster. Train regularly with weights and your muscles will react accordingly. Stop all activities and a muscle hypertrophy will slowly disappear.

The layman can get an idea of how a former athlete can become fat by the following example. Imagine a hard-training boxer working out daily for an upcoming championship title. He jumps rope half an hour daily. He does weight training. He practises the fast bag. He spars several rounds each day. And in order to find the energy for all this activity, he needs food—loads of it—not only for energy, but for recuperation and the repair of muscles and cellular tissue. He eats an abundance of carbohydrates, protein, and fats, but it's all used up, so there is no gaining of superfluous weight. After the fight, win or lose, he quits training, but he neglects to cut down on his food intake. An eating habit formed when there was a positive use for the fuel is continued when there is no longer a physical need and an excess of calories is stored on the body as fat!

The lesson is simple. When you cut down on training or stop exercise altogether you should also reduce your food intake. In that way you will keep your weight normal. Muscle cannot turn into fat, but muscle can diminish (with inactivity), and it can be *replaced* by fat, if you consistently overeat.

Lifestyle

Many factors affect our physical well-being: food, smoking, drinking, drugs, stress, exercise, working, and our recreational environment. Drugs and drinking should be used in moderation if you want health and physical and mental vitality from your early days right through your 70's, 80's, and beyond. Smoking can cause lung and stomach cancer, hardening of the arteries, and heart disease.

Although each of us needs a certain amount of stress, too much can be destructive. It causes the heart to beat rapidly and the adrenaline to flow, which gives added power for action. People have done extraordinary things when under the influence of an adrenaline "rush." It's the "fight-or-flight" syndrome.

When prehistoric man first encountered a growling sabre-toothed tiger, he either clubbed it to death or ran for his life. The problem today is that, although our adrenaline can still be triggered, we are not always able to act as nature intended. You can hardly club your boss on the head when he accuses you of incompetence. Instead, you shake with frustration, your heart pumps fast, and it takes a couple of hours before you are back to normal. In the long run, this can be harmful to your system, especially when it is not followed by physical activity, which allows you to vent some of your anger.

Tension and worry are often beaten only by a very determined effort to change things. Great relief and added health result. If you find your spouse unbearable (or incompatible), then get a divorce. If your job is robbing you of your well-being and happiness, change it!

Being fit is important, and part of that ideal state is the performance of regular exercise. A strong heart is the result of regular exercise (and incidentally is a very good way of at least partially counteracting the harmful effects of stress).

Formal, strenuous exercise, done regularly, decreases the wear and tear of the organs, especially the heart. As this organ strengthens, it enlarges and the beat is stronger, allowing for a greater rest period between beats. The average heart rate is 72 beats per minute. It is not unusual for the ardent exercise fan to have a heartbeat of 55 beats per minute or less. Regular exercise also improves the cardiovascular system and improves the chances of avoiding a shutdown of the main passage to and from the heart by building collateral circulation through additional passageways for blood entering and leaving the heart.

You can greatly improve your self-image with regular exercise. People who exercise regularly often expound on the improved feeling of well-being they get from the activity. "I look and feel great. Now life is worth living. . . ." The net result of regular exercise is usually abounding good health, zest, and happiness.

Arnold Schwarzenegger in his prime as a competitive bodybuilder.

5 A SENSE OF PROPORTION

Have you ever watched an artist building a model using clay? The process involves adding or subtracting clay until the work is completed. It is a lengthy process and invariably changes take place in small steps. In time the work of art is complete.

In bodybuilding you are your own sculptor. Instead of the mallet and chisel of a stone carver or the modelling tools of a clay worker, you use barbells and dumbbells, lat machines, and leg units. But you are no less a creator of art than the artist working in wood, clay or stone. You have a responsibility. Your job is to build a physique that is proportionate, symmetrical, and in keeping with your individual body type and skeletal structure.

Seeing Yourself

Try to be honest when assessing your current physique. It is difficult to assess yourself at first, but in time you will find it gets easier. Very few individuals can see themselves as they really are. I have known "overweights" who swore they were skinny, and underweight individuals who were convinced they were fat.

Learn to *really* look in that mirror. Study your shoulder width, your limbs. Do you have flat biceps or a high biceps peak? Are your calves naturally full and round? What about the shape of your thighs? Do you have lat development?

Problems assessing yourself? Have a friend check out your condition. (Select a knowledgeable and *honest* person.) Maybe you can get this person to take a series of photographs, front, back and sides, both in the relaxed positions and also posed. In this way, you will be able to study yourself as you never could before. Remember, you need to know about your own shape and condition because you are then in a position to make corrections.

Body Types

People vary enormously in their natural structure and muscle shape. Look around any beach or swimming area and you will see what I mean. Compound this fact with the eating and exercise habits of the populace and you will observe an enormous difference between individuals. Some weigh under 100 lbs. while others will be three times that weight. Check out the large, thick legs, the brawny shoulders. Compare them to the skinny pipe-stem limbs, and the pencil-necks of the underweights. Some have perfect posture. Others have bent-over demeanors and are barely able to stand. You see large hips, small hips, big chests, skinny chests.

Dr. William H. Sheldon of Harvard University, a leading exponent of anthropometry, devised a way of measuring body structure, and identified three basic types:

1. Endomorph: The rounded, pear-shaped type, often carrying large amounts of excess weight.

2. Mesomorph: The naturally muscular and athletic type.

3. Ectomorph: The thin, nervous type who usually makes a good marathon runner, and has difficulty gaining weight.

These three types have different bodybuilding needs. Endomorphs invariably have to control their bodyweight because there is a tendency to run to fat. The mesomorph is possibly the luckiest in many respects. The body is naturally muscular, well formed and extremely responsive to planned exercise. The ectomorph is usually "touchy," talkative and highly nervous—a bundle of energy. The bones are smaller and seldom does the body have excess fat.

Whereas we all fall into one of these three basic types, we could also have characteristics of the other two categories. Recognizing which type you belong to may be rather difficult. For example, you may not be able to conclude that you are a total mesomorph but rather a mesomorph with ectomorphic tendencies, or an endomorph with mesomorphic characteristics.

Your body type is determined before you are born. You can, however, often overcome what you may consider defects. Needless to say, different problems need to be handled in different ways. You have to exercise and eat according to your "type." Many stereotyped courses on bodybuilding help only a few. Chances are if you are individual in your bodybuilding needs, you will need individual, tailor-made instruction.

Generally speaking, the mesomorph can work out regularly, and strenuously, and for sustained periods. The endomorph should train lighter and be very careful about the quantity and quality of food intake. The ectomorph has to keep the workout short, yet strenuous, and eat more; this usually entails eating up to as many as five or six small snacks a day rather than the traditional three meals.

Are There Ideal Proportions?

Good proportions are essential for successful bodybuilding. Build some areas and reduce others. Men, more than women, have a big problem with this. If a man has a naturally big chest and scrawny legs, he will often tend to exercise his chest even more, and neglect his legs almost entirely. Result: Even more of a lopsided appearance. Women usually will work their underpar areas severely.

Men who have skinny arms and heavy thighs, for example, should work their arms hard and regularly and pay less attention to building up the thighs. Women who already have thin, firm waistlines should limit the amount of abdominal work they do. Concentrate on your weak points. Remember to direct the most attention to the areas that need it, but don't go to the other extreme. If you feel you have perfect legs, do not completely avoid *all* leg exercises. Each area should be exercised, at least moderately. You should never totally neglect a bodypart just because for the moment it seems pretty good. Muscle tone requires usage; and you would soon find your good points falling behind if you neglected them completely. Weight training involves the entire body.

Knowing what is good proportion can be difficult. There are no absolutes, no measurements that are perfect for everyone. In fact, two people with identical measurements (chest, waist, thigh, arm, etc.) can look entirely different. We could take our standards from ancient Greek statues or Renaissance art but even these vary considerably in their proportions. (The Farnese Hercules at 6 feet in height has 20-inch arms, whereas Michelangelo's David, of the same height, has 16-inch arms. Who has the more perfect figure: the Venus de Milo or a Degas ballerina? Tastes vary from individual to individual. Men tend to concentrate on building arms, calves, and neck to the same dimensions. Women need not be so concerned with actual measurement, because there is a great variation in hip and shoulder widths in women. Rather, they should make an attempt at improving "line" and "shape," which, of course, comes about by limiting excess fat. Underpar areas like calves can be built up with heavier weights than one might use for general conditioning.

Taking photographs will provide your biggest eyeopener to working on your own proportions. Discuss the pictures with friends. But before you do, make sure that they can give you criticism that is both honest *and* constructive. (Incidentally, friends or strangers, unless they are bodybuilding instructors, can seldom analyze correctly by just looking at your body. They are far more likely to make a good judgment by studying pictures of your physique, and so are you!)

What measurements should you have?

It is impossible to specify for women, since there is great variation in bone size and formation. However, the following points could act as a guide for men:

Biceps: Multiply your wrist measurement (smallest part) by 2.10 (ideal), 2.32 (Herculean).

Chest: Multiply your wrist size measurement by 5.62 (ideal), 6.42 (Herculean).

Waist: Should equal 64 percent of chest girth (ideal), 70 percent (Herculean).

Thighs: Multiply knee measurement (smallest part) by 1.44 (ideal), 1.63 (Herculean).

Calves: Should be 69 percent of thigh girth (ideal), 72 percent (Herculean).

Bodyweight: Multiply your height (in inches) by 2.55 (ideal), 3.1 (Herculean).

Tazzie Colomb.

6
TRAINING SYSTEMS

In the 1800's the strongmen of the era lifted a variety of solid dumb-bells and barbells to build their strength. There was very little planning involved. The secret muscle-building supplement of the time was . . . beer. The darker the brew, the better. One billboard advertisement of this period depicted a man lifting a horse, and the caption read, *"Guinness gives you strength!"* This type of misleading ad no longer exists because today's U.S. Food and Drug Administration police companies that make exaggerated, false or misleading claims without double-blind authentic tests to substantiate the evi-dence. Heavy fines, and even prison sentences can and often are levied at unscrupulous traders.

Today we have dozens of training methods, admittedly some better than others, but even the lowliest have something unique and different to offer the bodybuilder. At one time (in the 50's and 60's) there was a veritable war between rival bodybuilding magazine publishers, each claiming to have invented *the* best training system. Actually, these publishers had invented nothing but *names* for the various ways of training with progressive resistance exercise. The actual methods had been used many years

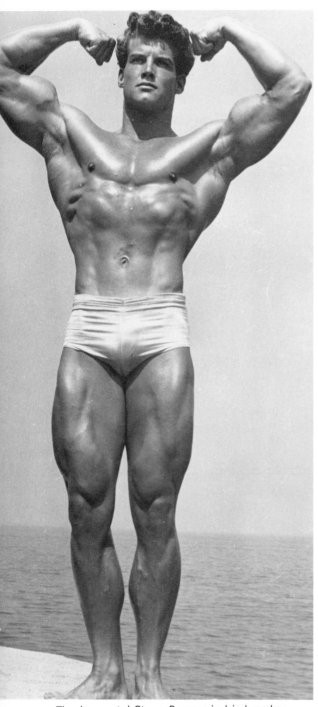

The immortal Steve Reeves in his heyday.

earlier, in most cases even before the publishers were born.

The Weider Camp, run by muscle entrepreneur Joe Weider, claimed that people like Clancy Ross, Leo Robert, Jack Delinger and Reg Park had the world's greatest physiques—and that these physiques were built with Weider principles. Most commonly promoted were the cheating system, supersets, giant sets, instinctive training and peak contraction.

The York Barbell Company, under the control of self-proclaimed world's healthiest man Bob Hoffman, pushed men like John Grimek, its figurehead for some fifty years, as being the world's best built human being. The principles the company advocated were the use of Olympic lifting to increase basic mass and strength, strict (no cheating) exercise form, and the practice of a thousand and one forms of exercise to build a complete physique. Grimek was depicted performing all types of unusual exercises, even some showing him hanging upside down using ropes to hold his body to a horizontal bar.

A third publisher, Peary Rader of *Iron Man* magazine, claimed Bill Pearl as having the world's greatest body. *Iron Man* promoted methods such as abbreviated workouts, as well as high-intensity and basic workouts, including only a few heavy exercises, especially the squat, which was claimed by Rader to be responsible for almost every pound of muscle gained by bodybuilders of the era. Needless to say, Weider, Hoffman, and Rader all made plenty of money pushing "their" methods and each sold a variety of items to capitalize on the ambitions of bodybuilders throughout the world. The biggest hoax of all to my mind was the isometric era, where in the 60's Hoffman sold isometric racks to almost every YMCA on the North American continent. As proof of their usefulness to iron men, Bob Hoffman cited the sensational gains made by "his" lifters and bodybuilders who "trained in secret on the isometric apparatus." Actually, they had just discovered anabolic steroids!

Weider was more diversified. In addition to promoting his Weider boosters (bodybuilders who pushed his methods), he also sold a variety of krushers, weights, and pulley systems, not to mention his ultimate coup de grace, the anabolic mega paks (a steroid replacement system), which grossed many millions of dollars for the highly skilled business-minded muscle mogul.

Peary Rader's claim to fame was the squatters "Magic Circle." Ever aware that squatting with a heavy bar across the shoulders is few people's idea of fun, Rader marketed a painless circular contraption with straps that went over the shoulders so that squatting could be performed with as little discomfort as possible. Today, hundreds of gismos, contraptions, and apparatus exist, but few are taken seriously by the hardcore bodybuilder. Good basic items like leg press machines, thigh extension units, lat machines, squat stands, chin bars and Smith machines are very worthwhile. The following are some of the most workable systems of training that have been, and are currently, used by those men and women making the best gains in the sport of bodybuilding.

Straight Sets

This is the most common method of training, and arguably the most result producing. This is not to say that other methods are not useful. The truth is that the body needs a variety of stimulation to keep it reacting to training. "The muscles have to be surprised," says Arnold Schwarzenegger. "They get used to a particular system and then your growth cycle stops. Keep changing around your sets, reps, and basic training procedures."

Straight sets is the performing of one set of, for the sake of argument, bench presses. You perform your set of 8–12 reps, rest for a minute or two and perform your second set. After another minute or two's rest, you take a third set, and so on.

Once you're into bodybuilding, you should be working with 3–5 sets of each exercise, although there are a few die-hards who refuse to perform more than one or two sets of an exercise, making up the lack of time spent by dramatically increasing intensity levels. This heavy duty training gets initial results but is not practical for extended periods of time. Heavy duty training goes hand in hand with heavy duty burnout.

Mauii's lovely Marjo Selin uses a pulley apparatus for her curls.

Lee Haney takes his seventh consecutive Olympia record in Chicago (1990).

Supersets

The name given to alternating one exercise with another is "superset." It is an excellent way to pump blood into an area. Supersets work best when applied with very little rest between sets. For this reason they also score high as time savers. For example, if you alternate five sets of triceps extensions with five sets of barbell curls, you will get a good arm workout and a great pump! Add another superset by alternating incline dumbbell curls with parallel bar dips and you will have completed a truly Herculean arm workout. No one should superset with truly heavy weights. In fact, use moderately light weights when you first experiment with supersets. Later, as you become accustomed to the method, you can boost the weights to moderately heavy, but never go for super heavy.

Compound Sets

This method is sometimes referred to as "giant sets." It is definitely a popular method of developing muscle among both amateur and professional bodybuilders. Again, it tends to have the added bonus of saving time. A compound set for the chest would involve doing three or four exercises, one after the other with minimum rest between each exercise. A complete chest-training routine using the compound training principle could look like the following:

Bench Press
   12 reps
Incline Dumbbell
   Press   10 reps
Wide Grip Parallel
   Bar Dips   } One Compound Set
   10 reps
Supine Flyes
   12 reps
Short Rest

Repeat the entire routine twice, for a total of three sets.

Pre-Exhaust

After having explained at the beginning of this chapter that the muscle magazine publishers were all pushing their own products, principles, and training methods, and stating that in most cases little more was done than brand naming them and promoting an old method that had been in use years before (in many cases even before the publishers were born), I am now going to completely baffle you by claiming to have "invented" the pre-exhaust method. I did so way back in the early 60's, wrote it up for *Iron Man* magazine in 1968, published a pre-exhaust course in 1972, and ultimately wrote a book detailing the principle—*Savage Sets* (Sterling Publishing Co., Inc., New York, 1989).

Much to the surprise of those who know me, I never claimed that the pre-exhaust system was the "most awesome principle of all." No. It is merely a *different* way of training. Great results can come from its use, but I do not believe it is an all-year-round method. I like to use it for one body part at a time to "jolt" the muscles into new growth. To pre-exhaust *every* muscle group, *every* workout would be too hard on the body. How does it work? Pre-exhaust is the battering of a specific muscle with a carefully chosen isolation exercise, immediately followed by a combination movement.

Let's use the pecs as an example. As you may know, the triceps are involved in many of the recognized chest exercises and in most people they are the weak link. That is, when you do dips, bench presses, or incline presses, the triceps are worked hard and the pectorals only moderately. This means that your triceps will grow more rapidly than your chest. That's fine if you already have a big chest, but if you want to develop your pecs, the best way is the pre-exhaust method. Here's how:

To get around the "weak link" triceps, isolate the pecs first with an exercise like the dumbbell flyes, where the triceps are not directly involved. After a hard set, carrying the exercises to the point of failure, proceed immediately to the second exercise, such as incline presses or bench presses.

When you do the presses, the triceps will temporarily be stronger than the pectorals, which are in a state of near-exhaustion from the first isolation exercise. You are not limited by the weak link in the triceps.

A sample all-round pre-exhaust schedule:

Shoulders
Lateral raise (isolation movement)
Press-behind-neck (combination movement)

Chest
Incline flyes (isolation movement)
Incline bench press (combination movement)

Thighs
Thigh extension (isolation movement)
Full squat (combination movement)

Back
Chin behind neck (isolation movement)
Bent-over rowing (combination movement)

Biceps
Scott preacher bench curls (isolation movement)
Narrow-grip chinning the bar (combination movement)

Triceps
Triceps press-downs (isolation movement)
Narrow-grip triceps bench press (combination movement)

Calves
Standing calf raise (isolation movement)
Rope jumping (combination movement)

Shawn Ray of California.

7
THE EXERCISES

Stretching

Ever attend an athletic meet? For a full forty minutes before the various events get underway you'll see all the men and women bending, stretching, twisting and reaching. What are they up to, and why are they doing it to themselves?

They're stretching. That is to say the body is put through a variety of stretches to warm up, strengthen and progressively challenge the tendons, ligaments, joints and muscles. Stretching is the best way we know to prepare our-

selves for a strenuous injury-free workout. Most athletes stretch before competition, although admittedly the Americans tend to stretch prior to an event much more than European athletes, some of whom still feel that the habit is unnecessary.

I would be misrepresenting the facts if I told you that all bodybuilders stretch before their workouts. Many do not. Some never stretch, but because of the physical demands from exercises like lat pulldowns, squats, calf raises,

Tonya Knight.

stiff leg dead lifts, lunges and pullovers, they have a degree of suppleness. Weight training does bring most of the body's functions into play, and you will benefit greatly, but I believe that those who stretch before a workout will enjoy even more advantage, and certainly a pre-workout stretch will help guard against unnecessary injuries. Stretching keeps the joints clear and allows a complete range of mobility. Tendons shrink if not regularly put to the test and kept in shape. Ideally, you should stretch your muscles every day but this is not always practical. Try at least to get three five-minute workouts a week, and work only on attaining ultimate flexibility. These exercises can be performed before your workout or at odd occasions when you have time and opportunity. They are not tiring or hard to perform, nor particularly time consuming.

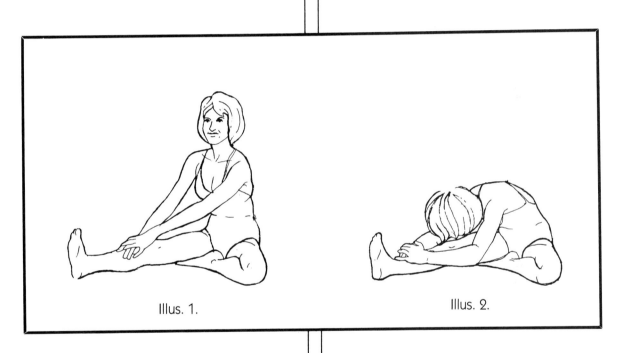

Illus. 1.   Illus. 2.

Alternate Thigh Stretch (Illus. 1 and 2)

This exercise will stretch the important inner thigh and help firm up the entire buttock area, while stretching hamstrings and all of the back.

Sit with your back straight, right leg fully outstretched, with your foot upright and flexed. Flexing the entire right leg, place the sole of the left foot alongside the inner right thigh and place your hands gently just below the knee of your right leg, one on top of the other (Illus. 1).

Take a deep breath, then, while exhaling, bend forward and run your hands down your leg towards your toes. Reach down as far as possible without strain (Illus. 2). Inhale and return to the first position. After performing 10 repetitions, repeat the same movement with the other leg. Try to keep your back straight and the extended leg tense, with your foot upright and your toes back and flexed.

Swan Lift (Illus. 3 and 4)

This exercise will work almost the entire body, with special emphasis on strengthening the lower back, shaping and toning the midsection, and general flexibility.

Lie on your stomach (use either a cushion or find a comfortable carpet). Clasp your ankles, keeping your head up, eyes forward (Illus. 3). Inhaling, pull on your ankles while lifting and arching your legs and back simultaneously (Illus. 4). Exhale and slowly relax to starting position. Relax in a slow, controlled manner. This is important. Try to pull your ankles and arch back as high as possible, but without straining. Do 10 repetitions slowly and completely.

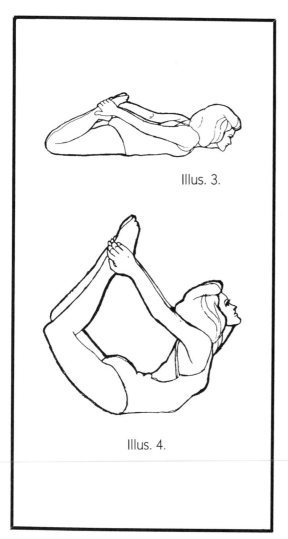

Illus. 3.

Illus. 4.

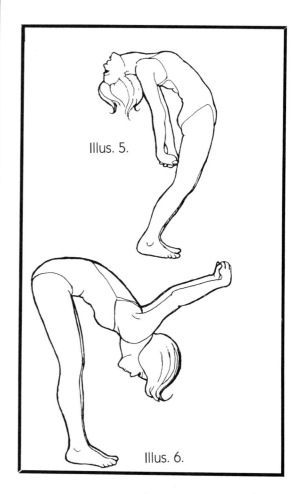

Illus. 5.

Illus. 6.

Spinal Stretch (Illus. 5 and 6)

Here is a really great flexibility movement that works the entire back area, while also stretching the leg hamstring region.

Stand with your feet about 12 inches apart and knees slightly bent, clasping your hands behind your back while bending the torso slightly backwards (Illus. 7). Slowly straighten and continue to bend forward until your torso is at a 45° angle to your legs. Pull your arms gently up over your shoulders (Illus. 8). Return to first position and inhale as you return to the upright position. Perform the movement as effectively as possible and be sure to keep your stomach in and arms high. Also, make a conscious effort to tighten your buttocks as you return to the standing position—this is an excellent way to firm them. Perform 12 repetitions.

Running in Place (Illus. 7)

Start by gently running in place at a comfortable pace. As you get used to the exercise, you may raise your knees higher and speed up the movement. As with the other warm-up movements, you should perform only until breathing becomes somewhat labored.

Illus. 7.

Illus. 8.

Rope Jumping (Illus. 8)

If you cannot perform this movement, a little practice will soon pay off. Many consider rope jumping to be the very best exercise known. Start by jumping the rope with both feet together. As you progress, you can learn to step it up in a marking-time variation. There are no rules to rope jumping. You can attempt "double-swirls" (two twists of the rope to one jump), cross over the hands, lift knees higher and higher, or simply increase the overall speed of the twirls. For the most effective rope jumping, obtain a ball-bearing-type handle and make sure that the rope is made of leather.

Illus. 9.

Illus. 11.

Cleans (Illus. 9, 10, and 11)

The clean is the action of getting a barbell from the floor to the shoulder level. It is a safe way of lifting a weight. Note how the starting position of the thighs and back is important (Illus. 9). Illus. 10 shows the bar in the halfway position. The lift is started with the power from the legs and hips and completed with the upward pull of the arms. Illus. 11 shows the final stage. The bar rests solidly at shoulder level.

Beginners to resistance exercise can warm up with 10 to 15 non-stop repetitions of the clean, using between 30 to 50 pounds.

Illus. 10.

The Shoulders

Your basic shoulder width is determined to a great degree by the natural width of your clavicles, but even a narrow-shouldered person can build impressive width by adding muscle (the shoulder muscles are called deltoids). Not everyone is aware that the deltoid is a three-headed muscle. There is a frontal part (anterior), a side (lateral), and a rear (posterior) head. For impressive shoulders you should exercise each area.

The shoulders are worked whenever the upper arms are moved and, of course, are strongly activated in every overhead movement.

Press-Behind-Neck
(Illus. 12 and 13)

This is probably the all-time most popular movement for size building. The lateral (side) head of the deltoid is worked most, although all three areas are exer-

Illus. 13.

cised. Perform 12 repetitions with a barbell weighing 40 to 50 pounds. Inhale before pushing up and exhale as the arms lock out.

When you get to the stage of being able to handle fairly hefty weights (about 130 pounds), you may take the weight from squat racks to make it easier to get to the initial behind-the-neck position. Some bodybuilders prefer to perform this exercise while in the seated position. This eliminates any leg help that you might sometimes unconsciously use in the lift. Grip the bar so that your forearms can be vertical when the weight is resting on your shoulders. Perform your reps without pausing, and keep your back straight during the exercise. This movement, although primarily a shoulder exercise, also works the upper back, the trapezius, and the triceps of the upper arm.

Illus. 12.

Illus. 14.

Illus. 15.

Upright Rowing (Illus. 14 and 15)

Start this exercise (gripping the barbell centrally, with about 5 inches between the hands), making sure that the arms are completely straight. A good starting weight is 40 to 60 pounds. Raise the bar evenly, keeping the elbows high, until the bar is at shoulder level. Lower and do repetitions. Inhale before raising the bar. Exhale as you lower it. Side and front deltoid heads are worked with this movement. Other muscles working to a lesser degree are the biceps, trapezius, and those of the forearms.

Standing Press (Illus. 16 and 17)

This exercise is sometimes called the military press because the body is supposed to be held in an upright, or military, position throughout the exercise. Leaning back as the bar is pressed upwards constitutes cheating, and takes much of the action away from the deltoids.

First clean the bar to the shoulders and then press it to arm's length above the head, as shown in Illus. 16. Return to clean position (Illus. 17) and repeat. Inhale before pushing the weight up. Exhale just as the arms straighten. Perform 8 to 10 repetitions with a 40- to 60-pound barbell. The standing press works all three heads of the deltoid, but mainly the side and front areas. If you can press the equivalent of your body weight, you are well above average in strength.

Illus. 16.

Illus. 17.

Illus. 18.

Lateral Raise (Illus. 18 and 19)

This movement is usually done with light dumbbells. Start with no more than 10 pounds. Designed primarily for the lateral deltoids, this is a favorite exercise for those who want to add width. Raise the weights to ear level and always keep your arms slightly bent. Inhale just before raising the weights and exhale as you lower them.

Perform about 10 reps. Some individuals prefer to raise the dumbbells to the arms-straight (above-head) position. This is entirely optional. There is no particular benefit in doing this. Vince Gironda, a pioneer in bodybuilding, suggests an alternate method for those who do not gain when performing the lateral raise in the standard way: Start in the standing position with the dumbbells touching in front of the body. The weights should be parallel. You will find that this forces you into a slight forward-leaning position. Now bend the arms at the elbow, still leaning forward. As the dumbbells are raised to ear level, turn the thumbs downward and raise the elbows slightly. If the dumbbells were a bottle in your hand, the action would be that of pouring liquid from the bottle. This Gironda method puts utmost exercise effectiveness on the lateral deltoid head.

Illus. 19.

Illus. 20.

Dumbbell Press
(Illus. 20 and 21)

The same principles and directions apply to dumbbell pressing as to barbell pressing. With the use of dumbbells, each arm is disciplined to work independently. The art of balancing both dumbbells simultaneously may seem difficult at first, but after a few workouts there will be no problem. If you perform this exercise with the elbows held back, most of the work is done by the side deltoids. Perform it with the elbows pointing forward, and you will bring the frontal deltoid into play. Start with a pair of 20-pound dumbbells. Perform 8 to 12 reps.

Illus. 21.

Illus. 22.

Illus. 23.

The Chest

This is probably the easiest area to build, because the large chest muscles (the pectorals) are very receptive to exercise. There is also an abundance of effective movements which work the chest extremely well.

Chest development is not only a matter of building up the exterior muscles, it is also important to build up and expand the rib cage. This is done by breathing deeply during each repetition. Lift the ribs high and fully expand the chest every time you hoist the weight upwards.

Floor Dips (Illus. 22 and 23)

This is the most basic and most frequently practised exercise for the chest. No apparatus is needed, although some people place (or have placed) a heavy disc across their upper backs. Inhale just before dipping and exhale as you straighten the arms. Floor dips are an excellent overall conditioner and definitely build chest and arm muscles. But continuous uninterrupted progress is difficult because the movement does not lend itself ideally to progressive resistance. You cannot easily build up the resistance on a steady progressive basis.

Illus. 24.

Illus. 25.

Bench Press (Illus. 24 and 25)

It doesn't take a genius to see that the bench press movement is in fact an upside-down floor dip. But it is superior as a chest-building exercise because you do not have to hold your body straight, nor do you have to balance to the same extent. The most important factor is that you can add small amounts of weight to the bar on a regular basis. In this way the movement becomes more scientific. Before you know it, you'll be handling respectable poundage in this exercise. Start with 40 to 60 pounds, and be prepared to handle 200 pounds or more within your first year of training. Inhale as you lower the weight; exhale as it goes up. (Imagine you are blowing it up.) Most people lower the weight to the nipple area, but those who wish to build "higher" pectorals may lower the bar to the upper chest. Under no circumstances allow the weight to bounce from the sternum (chest bone) as this could damage the delicate nerve center located beneath it.

When bench pressing, grip so that the forearms are vertical when the bar is resting on the chest (Illus. 29). Push the weight up to arm's length as shown in Illus. 25. Do not allow the weight to drop, but rather lower it with control to the original position. Perform between 4 to 15 reps. (Strength comes from 4 to 5 reps; muscle size comes from 6 to 15.) The bench press has been nicknamed the king of the torso builders because of its growth-producing effect on the entire upper body.

Lying Flyes (Illus. 26 and 27)

Start with 15- to 25-pound dumbbells held in the position shown in Illus. 26. Note: Arms are slightly bent throughout the exercise. This is to keep strain off the elbow region. Lower the weights to the position shown in Illus. 27 and return to original position. This exercise helps to build the pectoral area, especially the outer pec. No other muscles are involved to a great degree. As in the bench press, it is a good idea to breathe deeply during the exercise (inhale on the way down; exhale on the way up). This has a long-range effect of aiding rib box development. Do 10 to 12 reps for this exercise.

Illus. 28.

Incline Bench Press (Illus. 28 and 29)

The only difference between this exercise and the regular bench press is that this movement is performed with the body in an inclined position (an incline bench is "set" at anywhere from 35° to 45°).

More emphasis is placed on the upper chest as a result of performing incline bench work. Less weight is used in all incline work than when the body is in the supine position.

Illus. 29.

Illus. 30.

Incline Dumbbell Press (Illus. 30 and 31)

Both dumbbells are pushed up simultaneously, as shown in Illus. 30 and 31. Again the incline puts more stress on the upper pectoral area. Do 10 to 12 reps with 25- to 30-pound dumbbells.

Incline Flyes (Illus. 32 and 33)

With elbows unlocked, start this exercise with the "bells" held above the head and lower them until you reach the position shown in Illus. 33. Raise and repeat. Incline flying promotes chest growth in the upper outer pectoral area. Inhale on the way down. Exhale as you reach the initial starting position. Do 10 to 12 reps with 15- to 20-pound dumbbells.

Illus. 32.

Illus. 33.

Illus. 34.

The Thighs
(and Leg Biceps)

The biggest and longest muscles are found in the thigh area of the body. Probably the most popular way of increasing upper-leg size and strength, and certainly one which has enjoyed popularity for thousands of years, is squatting (deep knee bends). This movement itself is always at the heart of some controversy. There are two factions, and both have medical support and a wide following. One group states that squatting damages the knees. The other faction declares that squatting strengthens the knees. In fact, both may be correct. Do not make a habit of squatting "below parallel" with excessive weights; that is, do not squat farther down than when the thighs are parallel to the floor. In this way, you will not subject the ligaments of the knees to undue strain.

Your legs are the foundation of your strength and vitality. You often hear athletes—hockey, football, or soccer players, even boxers and wrestlers—talk of "losing" their legs. They know that, when the vitality disappears from their legs, they are finished as competitive athletes.

All the more reason to keep exercising your legs regularly. They are capable of enormous effort and can take plenty of punishment. Keep them strong and you'll be strong. Many people, even advanced bodybuilders, do not exercise their legs, yet expect them to be in top condition. This is not the case. Our legs often do remain in pretty good shape because we use them throughout the day, but an athlete must keep them in super condition. And that means regular progressive weight training.

Illus. 35.

Illus. 36.

Free Standing Squat (Illus. 34 and 35)

Stand with your feet about 10 to 12 inches apart. Place your hands at waist level (or clenched behind the head). Take a deep breath, squat down in position (Illus. 35), and exhale as you return to the upright standing position. You may place a thick book or plank of wood (2½ to 3 inches in height) under your heels to aid balance. You can work up to any amount of repetitions, depending on your current strength and stamina.

Regular Squat (Illus. 36 and 37)

The regular barbell squat is like the free standing squat, with the addition of a loaded barbell across the back of your shoulders. If you are very underweight,

you may want to wrap a towel around the bar where it rests on the upper back. This will help to prevent the bar chafing your skin. It is important to keep your head up and your back flat during the entire movement. Starting poundages vary from 40 to 100 pounds, depending on your present strength and condition. Many bodybuilders are able to squat with double their bodyweight. The best squatter of all time was Paul Anderson who, at 400 pounds, squatted once with 1,230 pounds!

One interesting aspect of squatting is that regular heavy squatting (say, 5 sets of 10 reps) puts such demands on the system that invariably the metabolism reacts and a growth reaction is set into motion for the entire body. Some authorities actually claim that squatting causes the body to manufacture far more of its own natural steroids.

Whatever the case, squats are responsible for more muscle growth than any other single exercise.

Illus. 37.

Illus. 39.

Front Squat (Illus. 38 and 39)

This variation of the basic squat is done in exactly the same way as the regular squat. The obvious difference is that the bar is held in front of the shoulders instead of across the back. The one rule is that the elbows are held high during the exercise. Starting poundages would be something less than those for the regular squat. Front squatting places more emphasis on the lower and middle part of the thighs. The vastus internus (the muscle on the inside of the leg just above the knee) is worked extensively with this movement. Perform 8 to 12 reps.

Illus. 38.

Illus. 40.

Hack Lift (Illus. 40 and 41)

Unlike the squat, the hack lift does not work the hip and buttock area. Virtually all the pressure is felt on the lower thighs. This exercise, named after the famous world-champion strongman, wrestler, and bodybuilder George Hackenschmidt is not known as a bulk builder, but more as a thigh shaper and definer. Use a starting weight of no more than 20 pounds and make a point of keeping the bar close to the back of the thigh throughout the exercise. As with all the other forms of squatting, it is also vital that you keep your head up and your back flat throughout the action.

Illus. 41.

Thigh Extension
(Illus. 42 and 43)

This exercise is done on a special apparatus called a thigh-extension machine. A somewhat watered-down version can be done using a table (or high bench) and a pair of iron boots.

Using resistance that is comfortable (about 40 pounds), start in the position shown in Illus. 42 and progress to the legs-straight attitude (Illus. 43). The results from this exercise more often manifest themselves in increased definition and shape rather than excessive size increase. Try anything from 10 to 15 reps. Start the "kick" slowly. Do not develop a sloppy swinging-cum-bounce style.

Illus. 42.

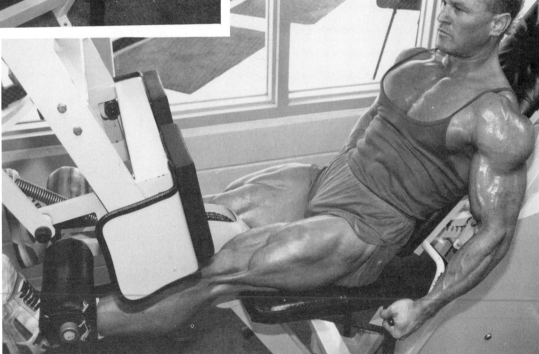

Illus. 43.

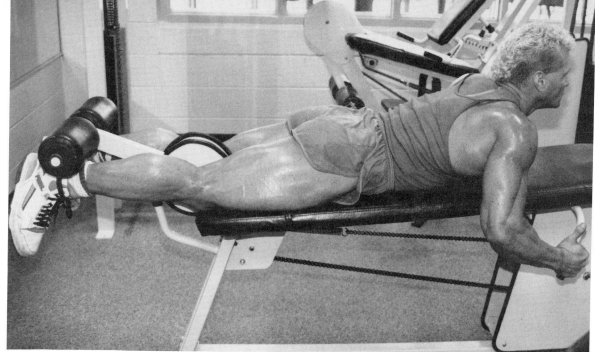

Illus. 44.

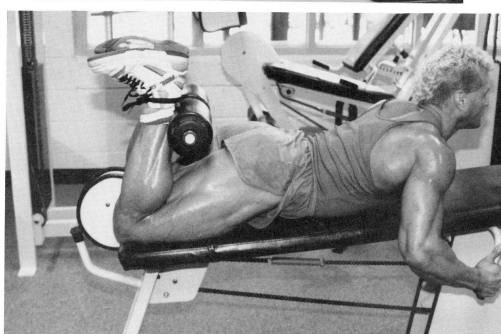

Illus. 45.

Thigh Curl (Illus. 44 and 45)

Again using the thigh-extension machine, but this time lying prone, work the thigh biceps throughout their complete range. Raise the weight from a legs-straight to a legs-curled position. Try 12 to 15 reps with 20 to 30 pounds on the apparatus. Breathe as you feel necessary.

The Upper Back

The back has some of the most impressive and beautiful muscles of the entire body. The main muscles of the upper back are the lats, or latissimus dorsi, which is the correct Latin name. These are the muscles that show under the armpits even when the body is viewed from the front. It is the lats which give that "V" shape to our physiques. They are the second-largest muscles of the body, the thighs being number one.

Illus. 47.

Wide-Grip Chin Behind Neck (Illus. 46 and 47)

This is a very important bodybuilding exercise, performed by just about every bodybuilding champion. Start by hanging from a high horizontal chin bar as shown in Illus. 46. Make sure that the lats are fully stretched and the arms are straight. Pull up strongly (keeping the elbows back) until the bar is behind your head. Lower and repeat. If you try to "concentrate" the effort into your lats, they will benefit. At first you may find this exercise difficult to perform. Keep persevering. Aim ultimately for 12 to 15 reps even though at first you may only be able to perform one or two reps. Inhale before raising up and exhale as the bar arrives behind your head.

The great benefit offered by this exercise is a wider back. There is a tendency for the scapula (shoulder blade) to be pulled outward. There is also a long-term benefit to your shoulder width. In fact, the wide-grip chin helps lift the entire upper body.

Illus. 46.

Illus. 48.

Bent-Over Rowing
(Illus. 48 and 49)

Set the body into the position shown in Illus. 48. Keep the back flat, and the knees slightly bent.

Hold the barbell with an overgrip (as shown) taking a grip width a little wider than shoulder width. The second part of the movement incorporates the pulling of the barbell to the waistline (begin with 50 pounds). When this is done, the forearms should be more or less vertical. Inhale before lifting, exhale as the weight is lowered. The movement builds muscle bulk into the entire upper-back and lat area. Do 15 repetitions.

Illus. 49.

Illus. 50.

Illus. 51.

Single-Arm Dumbbell Row (Illus. 50 and 51)

This exercise works similarly to the two-arm bent-over-rowing exercise, but there are two main differences:

1. It is done with only one dumbbell at a time and can stretch the lats to a greater degree during the movement.

2. The back is supported by the free arm. This is either rested on the thigh or on a suitable bench or stool. This lessens the chance of placing undue strain on the lower-back area.

Raise the dumbbell from an arm's-length position (Illus. 50) to the waistline (Illus. 51). As you lower the weight, make a point of deliberately allowing the dumbbell to stretch the lat all the way down . . . and then some. Use a dumbbell of about 40 pounds for this exercise, and try 8 to 12 repetitions. Like the previous exercise, this primarily builds muscle bulk into the lats.

The Lower Back

Ever since man first stood up on two legs and decided that he preferred it that way, he has had trouble with his lower back. Weight trainers do not have any more trouble with their backs than other athletes, or laymen, but it is wise to spend some time keeping your lower back strong and well developed.

Illus. 53.

Good-Morning Exercise (Illus. 52 and 53)

Start with a light barbell across the upper back as shown in Illus. 52. Keeping the back flat, and holding strongly onto the bar to keep it in position, lower into the secondary position (Illus. 53). Inhale before going down. Exhale as the torso returns to vertical. Try 10 to 20 repetitions. This exercise trains the important lower-lumbar region, and has a beneficial effect on the legs and hamstring area at the back of the thighs.

Illus. 52.

Illus. 54.

Illus. 55.

Prone Hyper-Extension
(Illus. 54 and 55)

This exercise is best done on a special apparatus as shown, but it can also be performed on a padded high bench or table. Someone will have to hold your legs in position, or you will tip over. Try lifting the upper body as high as you can and work up to doing 15 to 20 repetitions.

The Neck

The neck is very easy to develop. It responds to formal exercise very swiftly. For this reason there is seldom any reason to perform specific neck exercises since almost every weight-training movement affects the neck to some degree.

However, a strong neck can be very useful. Many a life has been saved by virtue of a strongly developed neck. Of course, it's no guarantee that you won't be injured if you have a car accident, but a strong neck is better than a weak neck.

Illus. 57.

Neck Raise (Illus. 56 and 57)

A special neck harness is used to add resistance, as shown. Start with the head in the down position, supporting the upper body with the hands on the thighs. Raise and lower the head slowly using a weight of around 5 pounds. Aim for 15 repetitions.

Illus. 56.

The Lower Legs

The calf muscles are important to build for overall proportion. Few things look worse than a man with a splendid set of torso and arm muscles and noticeably underdeveloped lower legs. No one wants scrawny calves, yet many bodybuilders, usually through neglect, are greatly lacking in this area. It seems that it's more fun to work the arms, chest, or shoulders than the calves, and the muscle that is not exercised regularly lags behind. Do not make this mistake. Your lower legs should be worked as regularly as any other muscle group.

Illus. 59.

Illus. 58.

Donkey Calf Raise
(Illus. 58 and 59)

No weights are needed for this exercise since the resistance is provided by a partner who sits on your lower back. Adopt a position as shown in Illus. 58. Move up and down on the toes, breathing as and when you wish. You can get a better stretch to the calf muscles if you place a block of wood (2 to 4 inches) under the toes. Always stretch up as high as possible when lifting the heels and stretch down as far as possible when you lower them. You will notice a definite burn in the calf muscles after performing this exercise. After a few weeks you should be able to perform at least 25 reps with a heavy partner sitting on your back.

Standing Calf Raise (Illus. 60 and 61)

This exercise also involves the simple process of rising up on your toes (lifting the heels). The resistance can be supplied by a special apparatus (a standing calf machine) or a heavy barbell across the shoulders. Again use a block under the toes and rise up as high as possible. S-T-R-E-T-C-H. Go for 15 reps with a 100-pound barbell.

Illus. 61.

Illus. 60.

Illus. 62.

Seated Calf Raise
(Illus. 62 and 63)

This is an advanced exercise which is usually performed on a special seated-calf machine. An alternative is to have someone place a heavy barbell across your knees (make sure you have padding).

Move up and down, using about 100 pounds of resistance. This exercise builds thickness in the soleus area of the calf.

Illus. 63.

The Upper Arms
(Triceps and Biceps)

Nothing excites the imagination more than the thought of developing big arms. Is it not the arms which are most exposed when you are dressed in a short-sleeve shirt, a T-shirt, or a tank top? Building your arms is a satisfying pastime because increases are often noticeable. When bodybuilders get together, they most often talk about gains in terms of arm-size increase. One usually works the arms at or near the end of the workout. Finishing your workout with a good arm pump is psychologically and physically stimulating.

Illus. 64.

Narrow-Grip Triceps Bench Press (Illus. 64 and 65)

The triceps is the three-headed muscle at the back of the upper arm. It has a fantastic strength potential and accordingly is capable of a huge amount of work.

In Illus. 64 you see the starting position for this exercise. Use about 40 pounds to start. Inhale before pushing the weight up. Exhale as you straighten your arms. Lower and repeat for 8 to 10 reps.

This exercise is always performed on a flat bench. The hands should be about 2 inches apart. Do not bounce the weight on the chest.

Illus. 65.

Illus. 66.

Lying Triceps Curl
(Illus. 66 and 67)

This exercise builds more size into the triceps than any other single movement. Lie on a flat bench, holding a 20-pound barbell, with your hands from 2 to 10 inches apart. Inhale before the lift. Exhale as the arms straighten. Try 12 reps.

Illus. 67.

Bent-Over Triceps Extension (Illus. 68 and 69)

Hold a 5-pound dumbbell in the bent-over position shown in Illus. 68. The action of the exercise involves the simple extension of the arm (Illus. 69). Breathe as you feel the need. The exercise is not demanding enough to merit deep breathing for every repetition. Do 10 to 15 repetitions.

Illus. 70.

Single-Arm Extension (Illus. 70 and 71)

This exercise is like the last movement in that the upper arm is held close to the head and resistance is extended to arm's length above the head. However, because only one dumbbell is used at a time, it may be lowered to the opposite side of the head, and consequently a new variation of this triceps exercise is brought into play.

Start with the dumbbell held as shown in Illus. 70. Extend the dumbbell upwards slowly, concentrating on keeping the upper arm close to the head. Start with a 10-pound dumbbell working up to 10 or 15 repetitions.

Do not allow the weight to bounce out of the low position, as this could damage the elbow.

Illus. 71.

Illus. 73.

Standing Triceps Extension (Illus. 72 and 73)

This exercise works the triceps muscle lower down the arm (near the elbow). Take the position shown in Illus. 72. The bar should be loaded to no more than 25 pounds. It is important that, as you raise the barbell, the upper arms be held fairly close to your head. Check your form in a mirror to make sure they remain upright. It's harder than you think. Inhale before raising the bar and exhale as the arms lock out straight.

You will notice that this exercise is being performed with a bar that has a couple of bends in it. This is called an E-Z curl bar, and the various bends are to enable hand placements which differ from the usual. Because of this difference, the effect on the arms is also different. In this exercise, an E-Z curl bar is used for yet another reason—comfort. The shortness and particular central camber are ideal for this movement.

Illus. 72.

Exhale each time as the arms straighten. This is one of the best pumping triceps exercises and one which many famous bodybuilders use at the completion of their triceps routine.

Illus. 74.

Triceps Push-Downs
(Illus. 74 and 75)

This exercise can be done only on a special pulley machine. The short bar is held as shown in Illus. 74. Keep the elbows tight into the body and the feet about a foot apart on the floor. Take a deep breath and push the bar downward against the up-pulling resistance.

Allow the weight to slowly pull the forearms up again and repeat the effort 10 to 15 times.

Illus. 75.

Illus. 76.

The Upper Arms
(Biceps)

The biceps, although smaller than the triceps, is known as "the muscle." It is probably the very first muscle you were aware of. "Show us your muscles," say your friends, when in fact they mean that lump in your upper arm—the biceps. For every inch of size on the arms, it is usual to gain 10 to 12 pounds in body weight; if you are having a tough time building your arms, you should make a determined effort to add bodyweight.

Many champion bodybuilders have started weight training with upper arms measuring little more than 10 inches around, only to find that, as the weeks turned into months, their arms were taking on a brand-new appearance. It always seems that everyone, even the champs, want to develop bigger biceps. Here's how:

Barbell Curl (Illus. 76 and 77)

Stand with legs comfortably apart, holding a barbell loaded to about 40 pounds. Your grip should be about shoulder width, or perhaps slightly wider (Illus. 76). Without leaning back, take a deep breath and "curl" the barbell to the shoulders as shown in Illus. 77. Do not bend the knees; try to raise the weight while keeping your elbows fairly close to your body. Exhale as the bar arrives at your shoulder level; lower at the same speed at which you raised it, and repeat. Try for 10 repetitions. This is the most basic of all biceps exercises and is the best one for building up that muscle.

Illus. 77.

Illus. 78.

Illus. 79.

E-Z Bar Curl (Illus. 78 and 79)

All the principles of style, breathing, and general execution advised in the previous exercise also apply to the E-Z bar curl.

The camber allows the weight to be held in a more "natural" position than the straight bar, and therefore exercises the biceps from a slightly different angle.

Seated Dumbbell Curl
(Illus. 80 and 81)

This is another variation of the regular curl. Start in a seated position, with the arms straight down at your sides. Curl both weights (about 20 pounds each) simultaneously to the position in Illus. 81. Inhale before starting the lift and exhale as the dumbbells arrive at the shoulders. As they come up, make a deliberate effort to turn the bells outward (the little fingers to face towards your shoulders). Lower and repeat. Try 10 repetitions. The seated position eliminates any unconscious cheating effect the legs and hips may give to the exercise.

Illus. 81.

Illus. 80.

Illus. 82.

curl and exhale as the bar comes to the chin. Start with about 30 pounds. After a while it is a good idea to really tense your biceps and squeeze the bar tightly when it is at this "top" position.

Always lower the weight slowly, because this negative resistance can help development a great deal. This exercise may be performed with dumbbells if you prefer, or with an E-Z curl bar. Some even use a reverse grip (palms down) which brings more attention to forearm development.

Illus. 83.

Scott Curl (Illus. 82 and 83)

This is a very specialized movement designed originally by Vince Gironda. Because of the phenomenal results obtained from this exercise, it is commonly known as the Scott Bench, after the great champion Larry Scott.

This exercise immobilizes the upper arm so that the biceps are isolated in their activity. When performed at a 45° angle, the movement works the middle and lower biceps. When a shallower 20° angle is used, the lower biceps and the forearms come into play. And a steep 80° to 90° angle involves the center and upper biceps which contribute to a "higher" peak. Inhale before starting the

Illus. 84.

Incline Dumbbell Curl (Illus. 84 and 85)

Lying back on a 45° incline bench, start your curl with straight arms (25-pound dumbbells are suggested). Inhale as you commence the action. Exhale as the arms arrive at the shoulders. Lower at the same speed at which you lifted. Do not permit a "swing" to develop. This takes away from the action. Try 10 reps of this exercise.

Illus. 85.

The Forearms

Although the forearms are exercised in many weight-training exercises, they can sometimes be very difficult to develop. A lot depends on heredity. If you have plenty of natural cells, then your forearms will come into their own as a result of general weight training. You may, however, have long "baseball-bat" forearms which give the impression of a long skinny wrist with hardly any development until the upper part of the forearm. Then you will have to work very hard to obtain really impressive forearms.

Illus. 87.

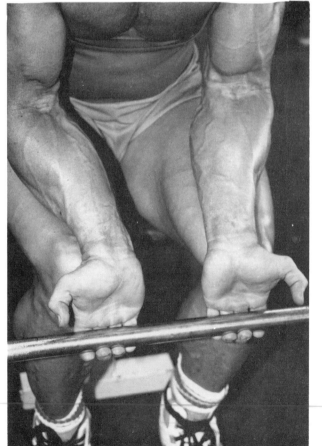

Illus. 86.

Wrist Curl (Illus. 86 and 87)

Rest your forearm on the end of a padded bench as shown in Illus. 86. Use a barbell weighing around 40 pounds.

Moving the wrists only, curl the weight up to the position shown in Illus. 87. Lower and repeat. Go for at least 15 reps. Your breathing pattern is optional. At the conclusion of a set of these wrist curls, you will notice a tightness in your forearms that you've probably never known before. The movement works and builds the "belly" of your forearms. You will know exactly where, when you have completed your first set of 15 reps.

Illus. 88.

Reverse Curl (Illus. 88 and 89)

This is very similar to the regular barbell curl. The mechanics are the same. The difference is that a much lighter weight is used (try 25 to 30 pounds for a start). This exercise also works the biceps, but its main function is to work and develop the upper part of the forearm. Try 12 to 15 reps and make sure that you keep your hands in a straight line with your forearms throughout the movement. If you do not observe this rule, you will find the movement virtually impossible. A final tip: Lower the bar very slowly. Let those forearms really feel it!

Illus. 89.

The Waistline
(Abdominals)

Because young people tend to be thin, they usually have waistlines that are relatively free of fat. As you get older there is a tendency to gain weight in this area. Both fat and thin people usually lack abdominal development. It has to be worked for. Do not make the mistake of thinking that 20 sit-ups each night are going to give you a fantastic waistline. Diet control is the basis. Exercise will help, but real impressiveness is lost if your midsection is covered by a layer of fat. Only a combination of exercise and diet will solve the problem.

You do not need to do hundreds and hundreds of reps when performing abdominal exercises, though some bodybuilders do prefer this. Nor should you do low reps, such as "sixes" or "eights." The stomach area is sensitive to excess effort and you could cause a mild strain. For most people, 20 to 30 repetitions are best. Bear in mind that a lot of abdominal exercise late in the evening could give you a sleepless night. Try to perform your waist exercises earlier on in the day.

Illus. 90.

Side Bends (Illus. 90 and 91)

These are usually performed without the use of weights. Breathe in cadence with your bends. Do not lean forward. As you get the hang of bending from side to side, speed up the action. Some trainers like to hold a dumbbell (in one hand only) to add resistance. After 10 to 20 reps, switch the dumbbell to the other hand. Those who practice the exercise without a weight may choose to perform up to 100 repetitions. This movement works the oblique muscles at the side of the waistline.

Illus. 91.

Illus. 92.

Hanging Knees Raise
(Illus. 92 and 93)

This works that hard-to-get-at lower abdominal area. You'll need a horizontal bar (or a doorway chin bar) for this one. In summertime, a tree branch can prove adequate. Start by hanging as shown in Illus. 92. Now, with a short breath, inhale and lift the knees as shown in Illus. 93. Exhale, lower slowly, and repeat. Try 10 repetitions at first and work up over the weeks until you can perform 30.

Illus. 93.

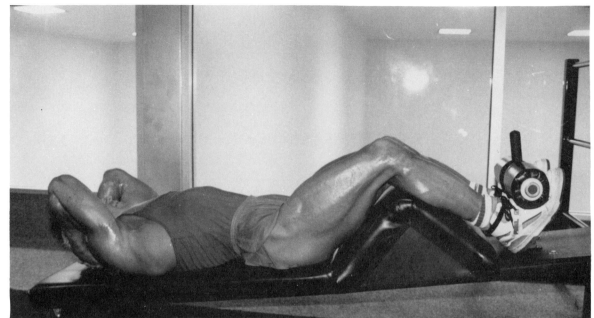

Illus. 94.

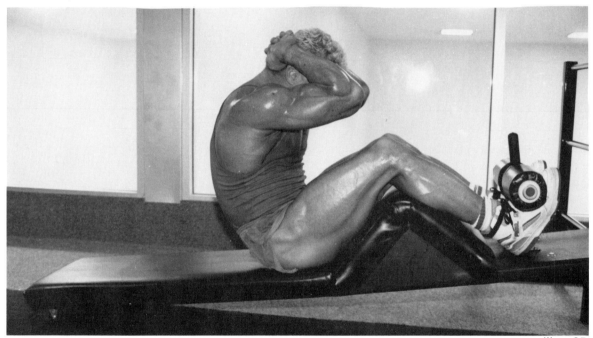

Illus. 95.

Incline Sit-Up (Illus. 94 and 95)

You'll need a specially made incline board for this. Almost every commercial gym has several. Remember that your arms should tilt forward as you commence the curl-up and you should round your back. It is medically advis- able to bend your knees as you rise; this keeps the strain off the lower-back area. Inhale before lifting up. Exhale as you complete the movement. This exercise works the entire frontal abdominal area.

Lying Leg Raise
(Illus. 96 and 97)

You may perform this exercise on the floor or on a bench. With a bench, you have something to hold onto, and consequently you will have more control over the exercise. Start, lying flat, and curl your legs up together until they are in the position shown in Illus. 97. Lower slowly and repeat. Inhale before raising the legs. Exhale as you lower them. The lower part of the abdominals is activated with this movement.

Hanging Leg Raise
(Illus. 98 and 99)

Another variation of the hanging knees raise, this movement is more severe and should be practised only after you have strengthened the midsection with the easier knees-raise version. Otherwise the mechanics of this movement are the same.

Illus. 98.

Illus. 99.

Illus. 100.

Illus. 101.

Bent Knee Sit-Ups
(Illus. 100 and 101)

Start either on a bench or on the floor. This is more advanced than the traditional legs-flat sit-up. In fact, you may find it impossible to hold the secondary position as shown in Illus. 101. Don't worry: Simply allow yourself to sink slowly into the original lying attitude (Illus. 100) and rise again. Attempt 10 to 12 repetitions, building up to 20. It's a toughie!

Illus. 102.

Side Twists (Illus. 102 and 103)

Simply twist from side to side (see Illus. 102 and 103). It is important to try and keep your hips facing forward as the body twists sideways. This movement is excellent for waist and hip mobilization, and can be quite enjoyable when performed to music. Start with about 30 twists. As the weeks go by, you could be doing a couple of hundred. Like the first abdominal exercise explained (the side bend), this movement works the oblique muscles at the side of the waist.

Illus. 103.

Simultaneous Knee and Abdominal Raise (Illus. 104 and 105)

Again, you may perform this movement on the floor or on a bench. Since there is a degree of balance involved, it may be better to start working on the floor. Be-gin as shown in Illus. 104 and simultaneously raise both your trunk and your knees so that they meet "in the middle" (Illus. 105). Lower both at the same rate and repeat. Medical experts claim that this is the most effective abdominal exercise of all. It works—if you do!

Illus. 104.

Illus. 105.

Lisa Lorio spots Cory Everson in the press-behind-neck exercise.

8 WEIGHT TRAINING FOR WOMEN

There have always been a few women around who weight trained. But they were definitely regarded as oddities. In fact, weight training for women can be traced back to well before Christ, to the days of the Egyptians, and to civilizations of early Greece.

Going back to the beginning of this century, a few women used bodybuilding methods to tone and shape their figures, but when the gym spa facilities and YWCA's began to emerge just prior to the war, very little in the way of progressive resistance exercise was available for women. To train with weights was a man's thing, exclusively. That was the thinking of the day. Any women who did train at this time were either married to a bodybuilder, or had a boyfriend who trained with weights. It was the only way they could get introduced to training.

The British were at the forefront of women's bodybuilding. Back in the Fifties they held the Nabba Mr. and Miss Britain contests. In most cases the entrants to the Miss Britain were related to (or close friends with) the Mr. Britain contestants, and, of course, they all trained with weights. Gradually the word got out and before long body-building for women was strongly established in Britain. Oscar Heidenstam, president of Nabba (National Amateur Bodybuilders Association), started a Ms. Bikini contest to be held in conjunction with his annual Nabba Mr. Universe contests. Again, all the women, without exception, were weight trained, and they looked it.

In the United States at this time a few women trained with weights, but the movement was pretty well lost to the public. Bodybuilding for men, however, was growing. It was Floridian Doris Barrilleaux who, as a trainer herself, encouraged her friends and neighbors to use weights, and again the results were impressive. Doris formed S.P.A. (Superior Physique Association) in the late Sixties and even started her own successful newsletter for women bodybuilders.

One of Doris Barrilleaux's star pupils was an attractive blonde named Georgia Miller. Doris entered her in Dan Lurie's annual "Body Beautiful" WBBG contest in New York, which he held in conjunction with his Mr. World contest. The entrants always wore high-heeled shoes, glitzy earrings and posed in a variety of adult-entertainment-type poses. They looked more like exotic dancers, go-go girls, or strippers. In fact, come to think of it, many of them were from those areas of the entertainment field.

Georgia Miller made history that day. As she approached the posing rostrum, she stopped, bent over and slid off her high-heeled shoes. When she stepped onto the rostrum, she didn't wiggle her hips and do the burlesque bump so commonly seen with the other competitors, but rather adopted traditional bodybuilding poses normally associated with men's bodybuilding. The audience loved it. The sport of women's bodybuilding was off and running in America. Ironically, the British, who had started trained women entering competition were slow to accept females on equal terms with men. Fully fledged contests were held for women in 1977 and onwards in the U.S., and today women's bodybuilding flourishes as both a pastime and a competitive sport. In Britain hardcore women's events didn't get underway until the mid-Eighties.

Many women have a dislike and even a fear of weight training because they think that they will build big muscles like a man. Curiously this talk frequently comes from women who are considerably overweight.

No, weight training does not build big muscles in women. It's impossible. What does happen is that a thin woman will gain some muscle size and a fat woman will lose fat. Weight training is the great equalizer. It helps you normalize your bodyweight. The average woman could not build large masculine-looking muscles simply because she does not possess the quantities of testosterone (the male hormone) required to build oversized muscles. In fact, women who are naturally heavily built (whether they exercise or not) invariably possess masculine traits and a possible hormone imbalance.

Regrettably those women bodybuilders who develop great muscle mass and definition are the product of artificial hormones that they have deliberately taken to enhance muscularity. Shot putters, cyclists, hurdlers, sprinters, and athletes in all fields routinely take anabolic steroids. It is a regrettable fact of life. The Olympic organizers have installed drug testing to fight the problem, but many athletes (especially with the resources of their government-sponsored sports physicians) are able to "beat" the tests by taking various masking agents.

Sensible weight training will tone up every major muscle in your body. It will improve strength, fitness and shape. In fact, you will look fabulous. Do not start your workouts by using heavy weights to begin. In time heavier poundage will become natural. That's what bodybuilding is all about. You become more adept at handling more poundage and everything about your physique changes for the better. As your fitness and strength increase, you will feel a natural urge to add even more weight discs to the resistance you are using. Go ahead, providing of course, you always train using strict exercise form.

Basically, when you lift a weight, the up-down movement should by rhythmical, travelling up and down at more or less the same speed. Take a short, quick breath between each repetition to allow a steady supply of oxygen into the system, thus preventing any possibility of dizziness. Normal breathing between reps also acts to pace your repetitions.

There are no exercises that are strictly the domain of either the male or female sex. The principal difference between men and women is simply that the man is genetically set up in a way that allows him to possess greater muscle mass in the upper body and arms than a woman. (This is not so obvious in the leg and hip areas where many women are better developed.) Another difference is that men's average body fat percentage is about 10 percent lower than women's.

Bodybuilding results are greatly dependent on nutrition. A woman can add or lose muscle weight (as well as fat) by increasing or decreasing her caloric intake. The ultimate shape you attain will be equally dependent on your calorie balance as on your weight training workouts. Too many calories and your body will lose the naturally attractive curves of muscle. Conversely, too few calories can give an unattractive stringy appearance. Do not be impatient to see results. They will come, but only in proportion to the amount of thought and effort put in. Remember that exercise alone, even vigorous exercise such as running and swimming, will not necessarily chase fat away. Restrict calories by eating less. On the other hand, diet alone, without exercise, will not do the trick either because you will not have the much needed muscle tone. Put the two together and results will be far more positive.

Take your workouts with a day's rest in between. A common schedule of training is to exercise Mondays, Wednesdays and Fridays. Do not exercise with weights daily. This could be too much for your system and you could end up exhausted. If you feel like being physical on "rest" days, go for a walk or run, play tennis, swim, or jump rope. Daily weight training is only practised by female bodybuilders during their last six weeks of training prior to a competition. After competition, most return to a schedule of three or four workouts a week.

Should you feel that one part of your body needs more work than another, do two exercises for that one area. For example, if your tummy is weak, you may want to perform sit-ups and leg raises. If your upper thighs are a problem, you could perform the lying side leg raise and the standing side leg raise. However, don't think that doubling up on all your exercises will automatically give you double results. The general rule is, especially for beginners, one exercise per body part.

Suggested starting poundages are given here, but even these could be too hefty for some. Do not be in too much of a hurry to use maximum weights. If you fail to start building well within your limits, you will get very sore muscles indeed, so much so that you may not be

Illus. 1.

Illus. 2.

able to take another workout for a week! Patience is a virtue when it comes to pumping iron.

Women who are seriously underweight may find some difficulty in adding enough muscle size, especially to the limbs. Frankly, if you are the original skinny-mini then you will probably never be able to have Amazonlike muscles. Conversely, if you are naturally big-boned and heavy, it may be next to impossible for you to develop the sleekness of a super-thin model. But don't get me wrong. The sensible application of progressive weight training, combined with a diet made up of the right amount of calories for your particular aims and needs, will work near miracles.

Running in Place
Jog up and down in the same spot. Try for 2 to 3 minutes at first. This is a warming-up movement and does not involve the use of any apparatus.

Rope Jumping
You will probably be totally familiar with this exercise; for many children it is a popular game. Rope jumping is in fact one of the best conditioning exercises known. Two minutes is adequate as a warmer-upper.

Stationary Bike
Riding a stationary gym or home bicycle can also prove a great warmer-upper. Three to five minutes of steady resistance pedalling is sufficient.

Upright Rowing (Illus. 1)
Start with a 15-pound barbell held in front of the body with a central grip. Space your hands about 3 inches apart. Keep your back straight and your knees locked. Inhale and raise the bar upwards, keeping it close to the body. Make sure that your elbows are held high throughout the lift.

When the bar arrives at your shoulder level, exhale and lower it under control to the original starting position. Attempt 12 reps and gradually increase the weight as you get stronger over the weeks and months. This exercise mobilizes and shapes the back, shoulders and arms (biceps).

Press (Illus. 2)

Start this movement with a loaded barbell (20 pounds) at shoulder level. Your hand spacing should be slightly wider than shoulder width. Take a gulp of air and "press" the weight to the arms-straight overhead position. Exhale. Do not lean back as you raise the weight.

Lower and repeat for ten repetitions. This exercise works the shoulders and arms (triceps).

Squat (Illus. 3)

A barbell loaded to approximately 30 pounds should be placed across the back of the shoulders as shown in Illus. 3. Hold it firmly in place with your hands.

Place feet approximately 14 inches apart and slowly lower into a deep knee bend. Keep your back flat, and your head up. When your thighs are parallel to the floor, stop the descent and return to the starting position. If you find it difficult to balance, then place a 2-inch block of wood (or two books of similar height) under the heels. Inhale before sinking down and exhale as you straighten up. Twelve repetitions are advised. The squat works the entire leg and hip area with special attention to the upper thighs.

Hack Squat (Illus. 4)

This is another form of squat; the only difference is that the barbell is held behind the thighs. The mechanics and breathing are all like those of the previous movement. Do not use more than 15 pounds on this exercise at first. Take care not to lean too far forward, and keep the bar held close to the backs of your thighs as you rise up to the standing position. The hack squat shapes the thigh and hip area.

Illus. 3.

Illus. 4.

Start the exercise lying on your back with a loaded barbell of about 25 to 30 pounds at arm's length. Lower to the sternum, the middle of the chest, and push upwards in a vertical line. Inhale on the way down. Exhale as the weight rises. Try 10 repetitions.

Good-Morning Exercise (Illus. 7)

Mainly for the lower back (the lumbar region), this exercise also stretches the hamstrings at the backs of your legs. Begin with a light barbell across the back of the neck (25 pounds should be quite enough). Spread your legs so that your feet are 18 to 20 inches apart. Now, holding tight on the bar, and keeping your knees locked, lean forward as far as possible, while still keeping your head upwards. Attempt 12 to 15 repetitions.

Illus. 5.

Incline Dumbbell Press (Illus. 5)

Start with 7½- or 10-pound dumbbells. Lie on an incline bench as shown in Illus. 5. Begin with both arms extended above the head, balancing the dumbbells. Lower slowly to the shoulder area and immediately push to arm's length. Aim for 10 repetitions. Like the bench press, this movement works the arms and chest. The steeper the incline, the more the effect is concentrated on the upper chest.

Bench Press (Illus. 6)

This is a super upper-body exercise which not only firms the arms and shoulders, but also greatly affects the chest muscles. This in turn can firm and raise the breast area, because the pectoralis muscle is greatly activated with all forms of bench pressing.

Illus. 6.

Illus. 7.

Illus. 8.

Calf Raise (Illus. 8)

Placing a 40-pound barbell across your shoulders, rise up and down on your toes. Stretch as high as possible on each repetition. You may significantly increase the degree at which you can stretch by placing your toes on a thick book (or block of wood). This greater range of stretch will give more benefit to the movement. Go for 20 reps minimum.

Leg Raise to Rear (Illus. 9)

Lean forward, supporting your body on a bench or table as shown in Illus. 9. Raise your leg backwards, as illustrated. Again, do not swing it up and down. The muscles must do all the work, and in this case slow movement is best. This is an excellent movement for firming the buttocks (gluteus maximus). There is also great benefit to the lower back. Work for 20 repetitions for each leg. As the exercise becomes easier, you may add resistance in the form of iron boots or weight straps.

Illus. 9.

Illus. 10.

Illus. 11.

Illus. 12.

Leg Raise on Bench (Illus. 10)

Lie on a standard heavy-duty bench with your hands holding one end. This will give you greater support and control. Raise both legs together until they are well behind your head. Lower slowly (under control) and repeat. Try 15 reps. No weight is used in this exercise. Needless to say, this is a stomach exercise. You'll know it for sure after you have done a few repetitions.

Illus. 13.

Side Leg Raise with Weight Band (Illus. 11)

Lie on the floor in the attitude shown. This exercise is made more effective if you wear a weighted band or an iron boot to add resistance. In this case, the illustration shows a Velcro fastener shot-loaded weight band. Raise the leg upwards until it is almost vertical. Lower and repeat. Try 15 to 20 repetitions for each leg. This movement works the upper-outer thigh, a problem area for many women.

Bent Knee Sit-Up (Illus. 12)

This is another exercise for the stomach. Lie on the floor with your knees bent as shown. You may need a partner to hold your feet down (or else prop them under a chair or bed). Holding your hands behind your head, elbows forward, sit up quickly and lower. Repeat for 10 to 15 reps.

Standing Leg Raise to Side (Illus. 13)

Stand with feet together as shown and, again with the use of resistance if possible, raise your leg to the side and slowly lower under control. Do not swing the leg. This would take away from the benefit. This is yet another exercise for the upper, outer thighs. Try 15 to 20 repetitions. Remember to work both legs.

Thigh Curl (Illus. 14)

A special apparatus is required for this exercise. Lie on your front as shown, with a light resistance on the machine (10 pounds will suffice). Curl both legs up together as shown. Lower and repeat for 15 repetitions. This is a great movement for the thigh biceps (at the back of the upper legs) and the buttocks.

Illus. 14.

Go for It!

Each woman has her own basic shape, thanks to her parents, but within her genetic limits she has a potential to be outstanding. Weight training can do it for you. It can change your entire world. Watch people's faces when they see the *new you*. If you are fat now, then diet will have to be a part of your life. Face it and keep to it. Soon it will become second nature.

Yes, believe me, regular workouts will transform your physique. The next time you go shopping, make a note of how people react to you.

How are you received at work?

Do people go out of their way to be pleasant to you?

Do you feel like a somebody wherever you go?

No? Then give bodybuilding a chance. Not only will you shape up into a dynamite appearance, but you will feel healthier. You will have vigor and energy. And there's more. As a result of your improved appearance, you will feel more confident. The world will seem like a new place. Excitement and adventure will be a part of your life, everyday. I have absolutely nothing negative to say about progressive weight training for women. Pumping iron will pump up your beauty and build that inner ego until you feel as though you are walking on air. Go for it!

Gary Leonard works his chest on the chest crossover machine.

9
GYMS

There are two ways to go with your training. You will either be setting up your own home gym or else you will have to train at a commercial establishment. There are pros and cons for both. A home gym is invariably more convenient because after a day's work at the office (or whatever) we have to return to our homes anyway. It's nice to be able to train at home on those nights when the weather is bad. On the downside, home training is seldom as result-producing as commercial gym training. Why is this? The answer lies in competition. In the company of others we work faster and harder. The show-off part of our nature takes hold, and we give more to our workouts. The net result is faster progress.

Setting Up a Home Gym

Ideally a home gym should be big with lots of mirrors and plenty of natural light. It seldom works out that way. One is usually relegated to using a basement or even a utility room. I knew someone who got a pretty good workout training in a closet. In my own case, as a kid I trained with a homemade barbell (plaster of Paris in large tin cans, held together by a rusty iron bar) which I kept in the garden. In winter I would brush off the snow or wipe off the raindrops, and take my daily workout, often in the dark. And I loved it. Today, I train in a two-car garage which I've converted into a workout area. I knocked out two sliding doors and put in a couple of large picture windows. One wall is totally mirrored and the others contain a variety of dumbbell racks, lat machines and leg presses. I even have my own Smith machine. I've always enjoyed my training and certainly my home gym atmosphere is conducive to some great workouts, but where's the ecstatic joy I got from training as a teenager in my backyard with those rusty homemade barbells, struggling for those three more reps, my mother shouting for me to come in the house for supper? Perhaps the difference is that in those days I was struggling to make myself into Hercules unchained, whereas today I am merely trying to hold on to what I've got!

If you decide to train at home, then you will want to know just what equipment is necessary. As with any sport or pastime, there is a multitude of bodybuilding items on the market. You most definitely do not need to buy them all. Think of all the camera accessories available to the photographer, yet a simple little camera can give you a masterpiece. Many people need only a simple barbell set and a handmade bench.

However, the serious bodybuilder, male or female, should consider purchasing a weight set which includes dumbbell rods as well as the barbell bar (usually 5 to 6 feet long). A bench, especially one that also adjusts to several incline positions, is also useful, as is a pair of squat stands to aid in your deep knee bend (squatting) exercises. And that's it! All other equipment is a luxury that you don't need, but may like to own for the sake of adding variety and interest to your workouts. In this luxury category are included preacher benches (for working the arms from a new angle), incline boards (for adding a new slant to your abdominal training), lat machines, calf machines (for exercising the lower legs with increasing resistance), and thigh extension exercise benches and hack machines (both are a rough substitute for squats, which work the entire thigh area).

There are other items available, but it is suggested that you keep, for the most part, to barbell and dumbbell exercises, using progressive overload methods. Free-weight training is best for fast, healthful results. Under the general heading of free-weight training are also included lat machines, calf machines, thigh extension and hack machines, for each utilizes the disc-loading principle that is so important for regular improvement.

Many people make do with very small rooms when they set up a home gym, but you should try to get as much room as possible. An ideal size would be 20 feet by 20 feet, but not everybody can allocate that amount of space.

Room height is important. You need to be able to hold a weight at arm's length above your head without touching the ceiling. If this is impossible, then all your overhead exercises will have to be done in the seated position. This in itself is not bad, but it can get a little boring. Another aid to happy training is a room which allows you to train in natural daylight, again not a necessity, but definitely advantageous. If you have to train in a basement or where there is no daylight, make sure you fit large mirrors on at least two of the walls. This will add size to the training area, and the movement in the mirrors will add interest to your training. Looking at yourself in a mirror while you exercise has definite benefits: You can study your exercise form; you do not feel alone; you are more aware of yourself and consequently train harder and faster.

A carpet is not necessary in a home gym, but an industrial or cheap indoor/outdoor carpet can make for more comfortable surroundings.

Always endeavor to keep the temperature of your gym at 60 to 65°. This will allow you to get the most from your workouts without overheating.

If the room is too warm during winter, open a window while you train. You will find that you can get along very well exercising when the temperature is low. You will feel comfortable at temperatures that you couldn't easily tolerate if you were sitting down watching television or reading a book. Besides, the fresh air will do you good.

Keep your gym bright, interesting, and tidy; place posters and inspiring pictures in it. They will keep your enthusiasm high. Remember to put away (stack) all your loose plates: Too many stubbed toes result when you leave weight discs all over your gym floor.

How To Choose a Good Gym

Not everyone wants to train at home. You may not have the room or the inclination. If you would rather train at a commercial gym, then there are a few pointers worth considering.

Most commercial gyms offer a variety of services. In some cases, the more you pay, the less you stand to gain, as far as real benefit is concerned. Of course, many people do not have a wide choice. There may be only one gym in your entire area. However, if you live in or near a large city, chances are you have a variety of choices. Remember that free weight training is still the best form of progressive resistance exercise. A room full of expensive-looking chrome exercise machines is not necessarily the way to personal progress.

First, visit your prospective gym at the time of day when you will want to work out yourself. Is it overcrowded? Was there sufficient parking space? Did it take you long to get there? (You'd be surprised at the number of people who join a gymnasium, only to give up after a few weeks because the journey is too tedious.) Are there plenty of free weights? Do clients have to line up to get a turn at using the dumbbells? Are there sufficient flat benches and incline benches? Do the instructors take an interest in gym members? Are there plenty of mirrors? Is there always sufficient hot water for the showers? Check out exactly what you get for your money. Some gyms close early. Others may not be open on weekends. Does your membership fee cover all the facilities—free weights, aerobics, apparatus, lifecycles?

Remember that the owner (or his salesman) has probably dealt with thousands of prospective members. He's an expert at impressing people. It is your job to see beyond the talk and to decide whether or not you want to become a member of that particular gym. Ask to see one of the gym's standard contracts—and then take it home. Do not, under any circumstances, sign up on your first visit. This may be difficult, because the salesman will be trying his level best to sign you up right away. Don't be surprised if the gym is offering a special rate that ends that very day! Above all, learn to deal with the salesman. If you are indecisive he'll probably say, "What is there to think about? We have everything, and at the right price."

Also beware of the gym salesman who asks a few details about you and starts writing them on the contract. Before you know what's happened, he's handing you the pen to sign. "We're going to do a great job on you," he smiles. Your answer should be one of the following:

1. "Look, I didn't tell you to write up that contract. I'm still thinking about it. Give me your card and I'll let you know when I decide."

2. "I'm not signing anything yet. I have a couple more gyms to see."

3. "I make it a point to sleep on all decisions regarding club memberships."

4. "I never sign anything until I have my bank manager check out a company. The last gym I joined went bankrupt and I lost my money."

5. "I have to ask my wife. She deals with all our financial transactions."

6. "I resent being pushed into any agreement and that's just what you are trying to do. I'll let you know when I want to sign up. So don't get pushy."

Many gyms thrive on the paid memberships of people who don't turn up. Don't be one of those who join up for a year and then forget the whole thing after a month. If you really like the gym, sign up. If you're not 100 percent sure, don't.

Eddie Robinson and Steve Brisbois.

10

BODYBUILDING CONTESTS

The idea of entering a body-building contest may not appeal to you. No one's going to make you compete against your will, but if your progress in body-building is constant there will be a day when the thought of entering a show will become a reality. The idea may not originate in your mind, but perhaps a friend will make the remark, "Hey! you're looking good enough to enter a contest!"

"Me? Enter a contest? I would never be that conceited" may be your response. But putting yourself on a stage to be judged for what you are is not conceit. It's exhilarating and fun. Anyway, there's going to be only one winner, and the law of averages dictates that you will lose more than you win. It is quite natural for both men and women body-builders to compete as they bring their bodies to a peak. Entering contests gives you something to train for and also allows you to measure your progress. It is no more narcissistic than playing football, soccer, tennis, or any other competitive sport. Here are a few tips:

- Never enter a contest "cold turkey." Go to a few shows as an observer. Learn the whys and wherefores of contests. Above all, ask yourself if there is anything the contestants themselves have to do which you couldn't handle.
- Assess yourself critically but sensibly. Obviously, if you enter competition, you do not want to be a total failure. Be reasonably sure when you enter that you are not going to stand out like a bad apple. On the other hand, don't be so overcritical that you refuse to enter a show because you are not perfect.
- Train diligently for a specific contest date. Remember that losing excess fat, a necessity for both sexes, always takes a little bit longer than we think. Most bodybuilders try to keep within five pounds of their best weight at all times. Start modifying your diet to suit your needs about two months in advance of the contest date. If you are overweight, you will need to really cut the calories during the last two or three weeks.
- Color is important. A natural tan is best. Be sure to tan both your back and front, plus your underarms and the outside of your legs.

If you cannot obtain a natural suntan, apply several layers of a good tanning makeup. Experiment with this prior to the event. Too many people new to the contest scene have turned up on the competition night with patchy, unattractive artificial tans. One woman inadvertently applied an orange makeup instead of a natural brown. One man put artificial makeup on his front, but completely forgot about "tanning" his back. Most black people should sunbathe too. The sun affords a richness to the skin that can only help your overall standings.

- Make sure that the bathing suit you select is flattering to your body. Avoid polka dots and patterns and keep to plain colors. Certain skin tones are suited to different hues. For example, light honey tans are complemented by sea blues and turquoise, and darker pigments, by reds, yellows, and browns. White is considered a poor choice for anyone. Blacks and browns should be reserved for darker complexions.
- Practise your posing to the point where you can breeze through it with hardly a thought. If you have to stop and think of which pose to do next, you will lose. It is the confident entrant who takes the top prize.
- Don't wear glasses during a bodybuilding contest. If your eyes are so bad that you fear you will trip over the rostrum, get fitted with some contacts.
- Men should *not* overpump their muscles. By all means do a little exercising prior to your stage appearance—a few bench presses, wide-grip chins, curls, and triceps dips. Don't bloat your muscles. You will lose important definition and, instead of looking hard, your muscles will appear soft and swollen.
- When entering contests, you are usually permitted to rub some oil into the body prior to doing your posing routine (baby oil is used most often). This highlights the muscles, but do not use too much oil. An overabundance can cause the body to "flatten out," especially if you are not in tip-top condition. Before the contest day, be sure that your oil mixes properly with whatever tanning agent you are using. Sometimes when oil is applied over an artificial tan makeup, the tan starts to streak, and you'll look a mess.
- Make sure you know which compulsory poses are required by the sanctioning federation of the event you enter.

From left to right: Lee LaBrada, Lee Haney, and Francis Benfatto.

• Finally, and most importantly, if you are not one of the winners, take your loss bravely. Remember that friends will invariably tell you that you can't lose; when you don't even place, they will tell you that you were robbed! Even audiences, by their applause and general reaction, are guilty of this at times. Do not enter any contest unless you are prepared to lose. If you feel you should have placed higher, then train harder; the next time you enter, you'll be so far ahead of the competition that there will be absolutely no doubt.

Posing

Posing is the art of displaying the physique. A bodybuilder who develops to an advanced level must be able to pose when entering competition. It can make the difference between winning and losing. Regular posing can also help your body's shape, size and definition. Next to progressive weight training, posing may be the single most workable bodybuilding exercise. Practice is the key. Study pictures of bodybuilders or video tapes; however, a pose that suits

Anja Shreiner of Germany.

someone else may not suit you. If you are short and have narrow shoulders, you probably should not copy the poses of a tall, wide-shouldered champion. If you are tall and rangy, you may not look good imitating the poses that have made a short, squat champion famous.

Very few bodybuilders indeed are able to display their bodies effectively. They can usually perform the standard "compulsory" poses, such as the basic lat spread, the side chest, the double biceps, and the front abdominal poses, but, beyond this, most feel uncomfortable. Many fear that they will appear less than huge and, accordingly, any deviation from the standard poses makes them feel insecure. But one in a million makes his posing a work of art. Not only is he able to perform the compulsory lat spreads and double biceps, but he can also flow through the more individualized poses. The best posers in the world include Negrita Jayde, Tonya Knight, Eddie Robinson, Mike Quinn, Lenda Murray and Lee LaBrada.

The crab pose, while possibly the least attractive, is also the most muscular: The poser crosses his arms in front of him and flexes every muscle in his body at the same time. Invariably this pose "brings out" the trapezius (on either side of the neck), the pecs (chest), and the shoulders and arms. Because of its construction, the attitude is usually accompanied by a variety of tangled and knotted veins that appear only in this position. Worst of all, the crab is so intense that only a few bodybuilders can perform it without twisting and contorting their faces horribly.

To become exceptional, you need to practise posing, and the sooner you start the better. In fact the body "grows" into its poses. At the beginning, performing a lat spread or a chest pose may seem pointless. Even if you are well developed, you may still not appear impressive, but in time it all comes together. Your lats grow into the pose; your chest swells to impressive dimensions.

Just as important as the poses themselves is the movement connecting them. Top-line posing is an equal mixture of drama and grace; it is art but appears artless. Only on close scrutiny does one realize the skill and finesse involved as the posing master slides from one attitude to another.

You can learn to pose by following a simple posing-routine practice session after your workouts. Perform poses for every part of your body. But remember that, when doing an arm pose or a chest pose, you must also position your legs attractively; this applies to every muscle group. Never show off one area at the expense of another. If and when you are in a contest, the judges will observe your entire body, from the peak of your biceps to the shape of your feet.

An amateur pose may often be flawed because of a badly positioned head. A wrong angle or tilt can throw off an attitude. In posing, you can be sure that, if it doesn't *feel* right, it won't *look* right. Try at all times to hold your facial expression under control. Smile, never grimace. As you might suspect, posing with an all-out effort, yet maintaining a tranquil face, takes practice.

Dieting for Contest Preparation

There is insufficient space for me to detail every step of contest preparation. I have in fact covered this in other books such as *Hardcore Bodybuilding*, *Beef It!* and *Reps!* (all published by Sterling Publishing Inc., New York, NY).

Generally speaking, one should increase training frequency during the last 6–8 weeks prior to the contest. Instead of training each body part twice a week aim to work each three times per week. Increase repetition counts by about 3–6 reps per set. As the contest approaches, bring your intensity up as high as you can.

Nutrition is the main part of contest preparation. Never throw yourself into a radically different diet. You will shock the system and put an end to your gains. Instead, begin your diet with moderate changes. For example, you could cut down on all sugars the first week, then remove milk products the second week, and so on. The secret to obtaining low body fat levels is to gradually reduce overall calories while continuing to train hard. Your main culprit is animal fat (found in eggs, whole milk, cheese, butter, cream, bacon and meats, etc.), so make a strong effort to reduce these by eating only fat-free cheese, milk, yogurt, and dairy produce. Cut off the skin from poultry. Check out products like bran muffins (they can contain up to 50 percent fat). Remove the yolks from eggs.

The last few weeks prior to your show will probably have to be stricter than ever. Eat complex carbohydrates (grains and vegetables) and high-protein low-fat foods (fish, egg whites and chicken). Avoid like the plague all fried dishes, junk foods, pizza, salt, sugar and animal fat produce. The 2–3 days prior to the contest, if you appear flat and stringy, you may carb up by eating steamed or baked yams (one every three hours is average).

This practice will fill out your appearance by putting glycogen back into the muscles, but take care not to over carb up. You could add fat. Continue to supplement your diet with a high quality multi-vitamin/mineral daily pak, as well as a daily potassium supplement.

Also, taking amino acids and choline and inositol (lipotropics) can help slightly in lowering bodyfat percentage. Your only drink should be pure bottled water during the last week.

Keith Whitley.

11

QUESTIONS & ANSWERS

Q. Can you tell me which is the best way to train my arms on a split routine? Should I train biceps and triceps together in one workout, or should I train them separately on different days?

A. The best way to group your biceps and triceps together on a split routine is the way you gain the most benefit. There is much controversy at the moment as to which method is the best. As far as the superstars go, their favorite methods vary enormously. Larry Scott, for instance, always prefers to work his biceps and triceps together, directly after his deltoids, believing that these three muscles tie in together. Who can argue with him? He has a pair of the greatest arms in the world!

Q. This may seem like a dumb question, but I just do not know how to breathe during my workouts. Is it important?

A. Yup! I would say without hesitation that breathing during your workout is pretty well advised! Now, to be serious, unlike when performing calisthenics, you should breathe in through your mouth, not your nose, during weight training exercise. Gulp the air in quickly and exhale in a deliberate manner, keeping pace with the balance of each repetition. For the most part, you should breathe in as the weight is lowered and exhale as you complete the "lifting" of the weight. Rhythmic, lusty breathing during your weight training workouts can help you lift more weight and do more repetitions than you would normally get with undisciplined, shallow breathing. Good, strong breathing can also help you pace your reps and avoid large oxygen debts.

Q. My stepbrother and I have been training in the basement with our own set of weights for almost two months. The surprising thing is that although we are both wild to build muscles, Hal poops out quickly, even though he uses less weight than I do. Also, he hates the feeling of working out; I love it. Why are we so different? We are both eighteen years old.

A. People are different. Most youngsters are in robust health and can get great enjoyment from vigorous exercise such as bodybuilding. Having said that, it should also be pointed out that before taking up a vigorous program of exercise, you should get a medical check-up and a comprehensive physical stress test. Some people are just not suited to weight training because of their physical makeup. Their bodies cannot tolerate the physical stress. Those whose families have histories of heart, circulatory or other hereditary health problems should also be sure to get a complete physical to ascertain their tolerance and suitability for strenuous exercise.

Q. I lack energy. I get depressed, worry a lot, and even my skin seems lifeless. Please help me. At present I do not exercise.

A. Your question is basically of a medical nature and since I am not a doctor I cannot give an authoritative answer. I suggest you get a complete medical check-up, telling your doctor your problem. If he says you are in good, robust health, then a good progressive resistance exercise program may be a good idea. Remember that drugs, tobacco smoking and alcohol consumption can all rob you of your vitality (energy). Your diet may be in need of revision. Eat plenty of fresh fruits, vegetables, and fish. Cut down on junky, synthetic food such as candies, cookies and other sugar-loaded products.

You may like to try the following milk shake recommended in Naura Hayden's book, *Everything You've Always Wanted to Know about Energy . . . But Were Too Weak to Ask.*

Into a blender pour:
2 cups skimmed milk
1 tablespoon safflower oil
2 packets (or equivalent) of any sugar supplement
1 teaspoon of vanilla extract
Start the blender on low and add:
4 heaping tablespoons powdered yeast
4 heaping tablespoons lecithin
Stop the blender, cover and put in fridge overnight. (The overnight

cold, for some reason, changes the taste of the yeast from awful to good.) The next morning, put the blender on high and whip till foamy for about 30 seconds.

Q. I want to build high deltoids that really look impressive when I do a double biceps pose from the back. I have a friend who has quite wide shoulder width. At least his lateral deltoids stand out well from the side, but he doesn't have fully developed "high" shoulders from the back.

A. The exercise that contributes most to building "high" deltoids when viewed from the back is the press-behind-neck, the incline bench, and alternate front raise with dumbbells. The muscle you admire is actually the frontal deltoid. Your friend seems to have spent more time on the deltoid work (lateral raise) which gives a longer look to the deltoid muscle.

Q. I don't have a calf machine at home, and I want to build really good lower legs. What do you advise? There are no gyms in my area, so I have to train at home.

A. Many bodybuilders train their calves with nonresistance movements like concentrated heel raise, and "burns." It should be pointed out that the greatest gains in calf development, made by men like Pearl, Park, and Schwarzenegger (all multi-Universe winners) resulted from many, many sets of heavy calf work using a machine. The best non-apparatus exercise for building lower leg size is the donkey calf raise. Place toes on a 4" block of wood, bend over at the waist supporting the body with hands on a chair or bench and have a heavy training partner sit on your lower back. Try not to do less than 20 reps and work up to the point where you are doing at least 8 sets three times a week.

Q. I am 5′4″ tall, sixteen years of age. My mother is 5′6″, my father 5′11″. I want to be at least 5′10″. My phys-ed teacher at school told me not to lift weights because it will stunt my growth. I would like your opinion.

A. Height is not determined by whether you lift weights or not. In fact, many exercises can aid a straighter posture and accordingly help your height in a positive way. Do plenty of chins, straight arm pullovers, pulldowns, and hanging leg raises. Do not do drugs or smoke cigarettes; both drugs and cigarettes have poisons that in some cases can prevent normal growth. Eat good wholesome foods, additional vitamins, plenty of protein, milk and liver, fruits and vegetables. Your growth potential is normally set at the time of conception. To a great degree your height is predetermined by heredity. In view of what you say about your parents' height, there appears to be no apparent reason why you shouldn't reach 5′10″ or more.

Q. I am worried because I have just discovered the wonderful world of bodybuilding but I think I may be too old to make progress in body development. I heard John Mikl, Mr. Canada, started training at 7. My doctor says I am fit and he recommended that I take up weight training to gain bodyweight, but I am 26 years old.

A. Dear me! Twenty-six years old! One foot in the grave. Now hear this! If you are in good physical health, you can make really fine bodybuilding progress at twice your age! It's true that John Mikl started training at 7 years of age, but another Mr. Canada, Vic Downs, didn't start training until he was 32. And he went on to win the most muscular man in the world award. An ideal age to start bodybuilding may be in the middle or late teens, but just because you may be older doesn't mean that you can't make super progress. But make sure you start right and don't waste your time on incorrect training methods.

Q. I am a serious bodybuilder and am wondering if I need a lifting belt. Does it help training? What are the advantages?

A. Wearing a belt for certain exercises can definitely help your progress. Use a belt for all squatting movements, rowing, deadlifts, and overhead presses. The wearing of a belt can protect your waist from overstretching. (When a muscle is stretched, as opposed to being enlarged via cellular growth, it cannot return to normal. It is like a coil spring that has been stretched too far.) A belt allows you to brace your waist against the leather rather than pushing to its own boundaries. Bear in mind that in exercises like pressing and squatting, a belt is a great aid in actually increasing poundages used. This, of course, invariably results in larger muscles in due course. You do not have to keep your belt tight around your waist throughout the entire workout, but simply keep it in position and pull it tight just before doing a set, undoing it afterwards to allow less restricted breathing.

Q. My doctor tells me I have a high cholesterol level and he says I should

give up some of my bad habits. I must admit I smoke fairly heavily (2–3 packs a day), worry a lot, drink beer every night and loads of coffee. But I heard that Sig Klein, Bill Pearl, Arnold Schwarzenegger, John Grimek and Vince Gironda smoked cigars. If they can do it, why can't I? Also, I heard that Mike Mentzer, Vince Gironda and Frank Zane like coffee.

A. Do remember that all these men live spartan existences when in hard training. The fact that they may enjoy an occasional drink or a cigar to celebrate an occasion is incidental. I assure you that none of the men you mention abuse their health. Grimek I am sure hasn't touched a cigar in decades. Vince Gironda does have a penchant for coffee, as I do myself, but even today he trains harder than most youngsters. Arnold may have an occasional cigar or champagne, but when in training he doesn't touch drink or tobacco. Your observation about Mike Mentzer is made to excuse your own bad habits. You pick on a few negative points of others, but you are the one who is abusing yourself. Two or three packs of cigarettes a day is not heavy, it's suicide. You should be walking around with a chimney on your head. On top of that you admit to boozing excessively! No wonder you have high cholesterol. You better get your life sorted out before you kick off from this planet from an overabundance of self-abuse.

Q. My aim is to get to the very top of the bodybuilding ladder. I mean the Mr. Olympia—no less. Currently I am training at home with vinyl weights, but in the mags I see guys training with metal weights, and the champs are often featured using Olympic-style weights. Does it make a difference? Surely a weight is a weight no matter if it is Olympic style, cast iron or plastic vinyl.

A. Each type of weight has its uses. Basically the vinyl sets are for those who want to protect their carpets at home. They are fine for the office worker who wants to build some tone into his frame. As a serious hardcore bodybuilder, you should throw them out! Ultimately they will hold back your progress. The same goes for cast iron. Use them until you grow out of them, and then go to the Olympic weights; at least for press-behind-neck, bench presses, rowing, squats and even curls. You may use regular dumbbells and barbells for most of the other "secondary" movements. Olympic weights, because of the balance and action of the precision-built bars, are the Rolls-Royce of bodybuilding apparatus. You want the best body, then use the best weights. You certainly will not become Mr. Olympia without using Olympic weights in your basic movements—nor will you get there training exclusively at home.

Q. I am 44 years of age, 5′10″ tall, and weigh 225 pounds. I have been training heavily for 25 years and I have enjoyed every minute of it. But now my goals are changing. I no longer want to be the biggest. I want to be fit, healthy and live to be at least 90. My diet consists of eggs, bacon, buttered toast and coffee for breakfast. Lunch: beef or cheese sandwich, soup. Evening meal: steak, potatoes, gravy, dessert, coffee. I train two hours, three times a week doing squats, bench press, flying, bent over row, press, deadlift, standing curls, lying triceps press and sit-ups. I do no other exercises. I drink

occasionally; I never smoke and feel all right. I look pretty good (big) but I know in my own mind I'm a little too bulky. My 32-inch waist goes to 39 when I *really* relax it.

A. It's time to revamp your training and particularly your diet. I suggest you go after shape rather than just massiveness. First, get a check-up with your doctor. Ask for a physical stress test. With regard to your exercises, I want you to start and finish your workouts with 10-minute rope jumping. If you can't rope jump, then learn. You certainly will not be able to do 10 minutes straight off if you are a beginner at it. But work up to it. I also suggest that you be a little more selective in your choice of exercises, especially since you are not after gigantic bulk anymore. Try pressing with dumbbells instead of barbells; perform the front squat or hack lifts instead of regular squats. Do wide grip dips (elbows out) for chest or incline flyes. Try alternating T-bar rowing with wide-grip chins for lats. Do Scott preacher bench curls (vary the angle from 45° to 90°) instead of barbell curls. Perform a variety of triceps work instead of just the lying triceps press, which builds the most bulk in the upper triceps. The same with your abdominals. Perform a variety: twists, hanging leg raise, incline twisting, sit-ups, roman chair work, etc.

You can of course return to your basic routine now and again for variety. Cut down on butter, bread, gravy and potatoes. Restrict coffee to two cups a day (or else only drink very "milky" coffee if you must have more). Start each day with an orange or half grapefruit, and keep sugar and sugar-loaded products out of your diet. I cannot guarantee you'll live to be 90, but you will lose your flab, get better shape and add greatly to your fitness and well-being.

Q. I am 17 and smoke heavily. I train with weights three times a week and am getting some results but not enough. I am worried because the past two months I've been feeling a dull, aching chest pain which sometimes becomes sharp, always on the left side of the chest. Could I get a heart attack from smoking?

A. Statistically you are on the young side to get a heart attack, although the pain you describe is similar to what one could expect from heart problems. However, a real heart attack is normally accompanied by other symptoms, including sweating, vomiting, nausea and difficulty in breathing. You have the symptoms for a condition called tachycardia, which is characterized by fast irregular heart rhythms. I am not a medical doctor and this question is definitely of a medical nature. I know enough, however, to tell you now to quit smoking. It will certainly lead to aiding a heart attack in the later years. Your doctor can determine the cause of your chest pains and prescribe treatment. Tell him about your heavy smoking and if he doesn't tell you to cut down or stop altogether, ditch him for another doctor who cares about your health.

Q. Please explain what the triple drop and pyramid training methods are?

A. The triple drop method is a system whereby weight is systematically decreased during a set to enable further repetitions to be achieved. Pyramid training involves increasing the weight each successive set and then decreasing the poundage each subsequent set. Both methods are enjoying a modern revival and both methods are used extensively by today's champs.

Q. My wife and I have always kept strong, fit and healthy with sports and light weight training, but now as we approach our forties we are finding that our buttocks are looking flat and soft. Can you give us some help in showing us how to regain the firm, rounded "buns" that we had in our younger years. Would a three or four times a week program of jogging help?

A. The glutes are one of the largest muscles in the body and they are not easily kept in shape, especially in the later years. Activities like running, stair climbing, tennis and skating strongly affect the area and will serve to keep the glutes firm and rounded. Jogging is a fat burner, but it does not serve to firm and round the buttocks.

Formal exercises, like prone hyper extensions, barbell lunges, stiff leg deadlifts, 45° leg presses and low pulley kickbacks, make the glutes rounder. To perform the latter exercise, stand facing a low pulley machine with a leather harness attachment wrapped around one ankle. Stand upright and bring the straight leg backwards in a slow, controlled fashion until it is almost parallel to the floor. Return and repeat. Start with two sets of 15 reps each leg. Work up to five sets of 15 reps each leg. You'll get rounded buns.

Q. I am 15 years old. I am in a period of rapid upward physical growth and am having great difficulty putting on bulk weight. Since beginning weightlifting one year ago, most of my gains have been small enough even though I lift quite heavy for my age. My muscles are well defined, but require more bulk. I eat a fair amount of protein-high foods and little fat, but this seems to make little difference. I would be very grateful for any advice you could give on my diet and lifting so that I can put on muscle weight and size.

A. At this stage of growing, where your height is increasing rapidly, you should make sure that you eat well (cheese, meats, eggs, milk, poultry, fish, vegetables, salads, whole grains) and eat frequently. Split your workout into two halves and train only four days a week, so that each body part is exercised only twice per week. Limit your sets per body part to 6. Reps should be 8–12 for arms, chest, and back and 12–20 for quads, calves, abs and forearms. Try a good milk-and-egg protein mix twice a day.

Q. I want to lose fat and look my very best. I have been on dozens of diets over the years, but after losing a few pounds I usually give up in disgust because progress comes to a halt. Are there any products available to help dieters? Please list some names and addresses of where I can order any products or diet books.

A. Mail-order ads for weight loss products are sometimes misleading. Beware of anything that sounds impossible or larger than life. The following are some items which have proved themselves over a period of trial and error.

Figura: Thermodynamic Weight Loss Course
A step-by-step program detailing the way to sure and safe weight reduction. $6 (plus $2 mailing costs).

Orderline: 1-416-457-3030 (Visa, Mastercard).

Dynamic Body Shaper
This plan reduces intra-muscular fat! Available in GNC stores or from Weider Health and Fitness. 3 lb. can (chocolate or vanilla). Toll-Free orderline: 1-800-423-5713.

Thyomucase (Imported from France)
A cream that bodybuilders rub onto the skin surface to reduce subcutaneous fat levels and increase firmness of the skin. $20.00 per tube (no mailing costs). Ideal for pre-contest preparation. Orderline (Visa/Mastercard) 1-416-457-3030. MMI Sales, 52 Bramsteelle Rd., Unit #2, Brampton, Ont. Can L6W 3M5.

Choline and Inositol Fat Burners
A derivative of vitamin B that acts as a fat emulsifier. $18.50 per bottle plus $3 mailing costs. Canusa Products, P.O. Box 125, Rockaway, NJ 07866.

Shape Up Your Waistline
A new course to help shape your midsection into a rock-hard showcase of muscle. $5 postpaid. MMI Sales, 2 Melanie Dr., Unit 7, Bramales, Ont. Can L6T 4K9.

Fat Burners
100 tablets $15.95 plus $2.00 mailing costs. From Ultimate Strength Systems, 2144 Berlin Tpke, Newington, CT 06111. Orderline: 1-800-722-FIRM.

Q. How can I strengthen my arms just for arm wrestling?

A. You should be aware that all the muscles of the body are involved in arm wrestling, not just for the arms. If you really want to excel in this field, you should work the entire body three times a week to add strength for your arm wrestling. Your back, shoulders, and even legs and abdominals should be worked vigorously so that you are conditioned for contests. You should also practise arm wrestling with stronger opponents (or two weaker opponents) so that your specific arm-wrestling hand is exercised thoroughly on a regular basis.

Q. I am going to buy my first set of weights. The sports store near me carries both vinyl weights and cast iron. Which is better?

A. Vinyl weights are kinder to carpets. That's about the only advantage. They are usually filled with either sand or cement, and can crack open if lowered heavily, or dropped. Also, if they are allowed to get wet or are subjected to heavy winter conditions, they may suffer harm. As you get stronger, you will need to use fairly heavy weights, and the vinyl discs are so broad that they take up twice as much room on the bar as cast-iron discs. As an investment, cast-iron discs have kept pace with inflation. There is no wear and tear. A quick spray of paint on a 20-year-old barbell set makes them like new. All serious progressive resistance trainers prefer to work out with cast-iron weights.

Q. I have a very poor self-image. Will bodybuilding help?

A. Your low opinion of yourself may be due to any one of a thousand reasons. Therefore, it is difficult to state categorically that a program of bodybuilding, even if entirely successful, will change your low self-image. On the positive side, many thousands of individuals have improved confidence and pride in themselves because of the spectacular results they have achieved from progressive bodybuilding.

Q. I have been bodybuilding for about five years now, and cannot seem to get a good pump when I work my chest. I have tried many different exercises and techniques, but nothing seems to give me the same feeling of strict isolation that I get when I work my biceps. Do you have any suggestions or ideas that might help me?

A. It would have been helpful if you had listed the exercises you have tried, the different training principles you have experimented with, and how long you rest between sets. Obviously, resting too long between sets makes it impossible to get a good pump in any muscle group. Try to restrict your rest time on straight sets to less than 60 seconds. And really concentrate on working your pecs, not just doing mindless reps and sets.

The best way to experience a good chest pump is through high-intensity techniques like supersetting, tri-setting, pre-exhaust, and triple dropping. For an excellent chest pump, try supersetting flat bench presses and flat flyes, 4×8 reps each. Keep rest time to a minimum when going from one exercise to the next, and never rest more than 60 seconds between supersets. You might also try a tri-set of bench presses, incline flyes and dips, say three or four sets of 6–10 reps each.

You may be one of those individuals who has a hard time isolating the pecs and you may find that in dips, bench presses, and incline presses that your triceps take over and do most of the work instead of your pecs. For you, pre-exhausting could be just the solution to your problem.

Do pec deck flyes before incline presses for four cycles or dumbbell flat flyes before flat bench presses for four cycles. Keep your reps between six and ten reps per exercise. Set up your equipment so that rest between your exercises is kept to a minimum (say less than 5 seconds) and try for less than 60-seconds rest between cycles. You may need to decrease the weight of the compound movement the last two sets in order to get in the necessary number of reps.

The last method I'd recommend you try is to get a good chest pump and do triple dropping, which is an excellent way to extend a set and greatly increase intensity (and pump). To triple drop when bench pressing, start with a weight you can handle for about five or six reps. When you fail with this weight, have your training partner (or better yet, partners) immediately remove about 15 percent of the weight from the bar. With no rest, continue pressing until you fail again, five, six, or whatever reps later. Again, they remove weight and you press until you fail again. Once more weight is removed and you press until you fail again. That ends the set. For example, if your starting weight was 200 pounds, your partners would remove about 30 pounds, at the first drop, so the bar would weigh about 170 pounds. At the next drop, they would pull about 25 pounds off the bar, so it would weigh 145 pounds. For the last drop, they would pull about 20 pounds off, so the bar would weigh 125 pounds. Make sure you arrange to have enough small plates on the bar so that they can pull off the appropriate amount. Later, as you get stronger, remove

Lou Ferrigno.

only about 10 percent from the bar each drop instead of 15 percent.

Give supersetting, tri-setting, pre-exhausting, and triple dropping a try. These training principles should really help pump those pecs.

Q. I don't know what to do. I'm 16 years old, 5'9" and weigh 195 pounds. I train on a three days on, one day off routine. While I've built my share of mass, I lack definition. My problem areas are my abs, thighs, and obliques. I take two aminos a day and I follow Weider principles. Could you suggest a few exercises and a diet I could follow?

A. You weigh too much. I think you need to lose 15 or 20 pounds. You didn't list your training routine, so I can't make any recommendations there, but keep your sets per bodypart to 12 or under for major muscle groups, 8 or less for minor ones. Keep your reps between 6 and 12 for upper body exercises and between 10 and 20 for lower body exercises. Abs can be trained for very high reps, such as 50 to 100.

    I recommend you start to do some aerobics: running, jogging, aerobic classes, stationary cycling, stair running, or using the Stairmaster at the gym. This will increase fat burning and quickly help harden you up.

    In conjunction with the aerobics and weight training, change your diet so that you cut down on fats, salt, and sugar, and decrease your caloric intake slightly so that you are taking in between 300–500 calories a day less than your maintenance level, or the amount of calories you consume each day to maintain your present bodyweight. Aim at losing between one-half pound to one pound a week until you reach the desired weight you want. When your abs are hard and defined, that should indicate the rest of your body is hard and defined too.

Q. Can you give me a couple of good exercises for the lower abs? I've got pretty good upper abs, but I badly need muscles below the navel. What should I do?

A. The lower abs are always the last to come in. Some people have no rows of abs below the navel to develop, just a sheath of tissue. To get cut lower abs, you will have to drop some body fat, too. Now for your exercises. Hanging leg raises is a great one. This can be done hanging from a chin bar or from the dipping bars to take strain off the hands. The key is to do the exercise slowly and pull the knees up as high as you can to get a good contraction. Try 4 sets of 20 to 25 reps. I also like knee-ins. Lie on a flat bench and bring the knees up to your chin in a curling fashion. Again, tense the abs hard at the top. Try 4 sets of 25 reps. For a real lower ab burn, try supersetting the above two exercises.

Q. Can weight training help me increase my speed in sports?

A. In a roundabout way, weight training can benefit you, but not if you perform only a few basic movements. Weight training conditions and strengthens tendons, muscles, and ligaments. This in turn will complement all physical activities when better performance is required. But you have to practise your sport in conjunction with weight training if you want to increase speed significantly. Remember also that ultimate speed (reflexes) often depends largely on inherited traits. Some people are just naturally faster than others. Strength training will help you but speed will only improve when striven for specifically.

Q. I have heard the word "specialization" used in reference to bodybuilding. What does it mean and how does it benefit an individual in his training?

A. Specialization should never be undertaken during your first year of training. The term is used when an experienced bodybuilder wishes to concentrate on one particular bodypart, usually because it is lagging behind in development. The mistake that many make when specializing is that they train an under-par area *exclusively* and neglect to train the rest of the body.

This is not how specialization is supposed to work. One should always perform two or three sets of exercise for all bodyparts when specializing—up to 15 sets for the area that you are concentrating on. One seldom practises this type of training for more than three months, after which a more balanced program is undertaken. Should you, at a later time, feel that you need to specialize on another bodypart, then you can adopt the specialization program once again.

Q. I want to improve my posture. I would like a simple exercise to do.

A. There are several kinds of posture defects. Some involve a curvature of the upper spine while others may involve the lower spine. Most formal exercises aid and strengthen the posture to some extent, but the single best "exercise" is simply to straighten up whenever you catch yourself slouching. A constant slouch creates, in time, poor posture. If you strive to hold your back and shoulders upright, then your posture will improve. We grow according to the way we stand, lie, and sit. Correct your posture whenever you think of it, and you will improve greatly.

Q. How can I get strength without a large increase in muscle size? I am studying karate and I want to hold my weight where it is now, at 160 pounds.

A. Perform the following schedule three times a week with at least one day's rest between your weight workouts.

	Sets	Reps
Seated dumbbell press	4	5
Flat-footed squats	4	5
Bench press	4	5
Deadlift	4	5

The above exercises can be performed in conjunction with your regular karate exercises, limbering and abdominal movements. Work up until you are using heavy weights. For the lean look, follow a high-protein, moderate carbohydrate diet. (To bulk up, follow a high-protein, high carbohydrate diet.) If you find that you are gaining too much mass, cut your calorie intake even more.

Q. I am interested in knowing exactly what weight training can or cannot do to benefit a woman's bustline.

A. A woman's breast is not a muscle but a gland. Therefore, exercises will not increase its size. Bustline exercises serve to strengthen the underlying muscles which can lift and *tone* the general bosom area. Also, bustline measurements can be increased by the enlargement of these pectoral muscles and the latissimus muscles (of the upper back), but the mammaries themselves will not enlarge as a result of exercise. Larger breast measurements will result from overall body weight increase and some women find that their breasts enlarge as a result of taking the birth-control pill, and of course during pregnancy. Women bodybuilders who diet down for contests tend to lose breast size, but this is only temporary. It comes back when the strict diet is relaxed.

Q. What is meant by Olympic lifting?

A. Olympic lifting is performed only by men at the Olympics and at weight-lifting contests. A handful of women practise the movements, but organized Women's Olympic lifting meets are few and far between. There are two Olympic lifts:

The Snatch: The weight is lifted from the ground in one pull to arm's length above the head. The individual may duck under the weight by either squatting or by splitting his legs (one forward, one back). In order to judge a good lift, the snatch must be brought to arm's length with the lifter standing upright with feet together, showing that he has control over the lift.

The Clean and Jerk: In this lift, the weight has to be lifted in one movement to the shoulders and then hoisted, pushed or jerked to arm's length above the head. Again, the lifter has to show that he has total control by standing upright with the weight held aloft for several seconds. As with the snatch, the first part of this movement (lifting the weight to the shoulders) may be performed by either squatting under the weight as it is pulled from the floor or by splitting the legs and ducking under the bar as it rises.

During competition each lifter is allowed three attempts at each lift. The highest poundage on both lifts is added and the sum is called the lifter's "total." The man with the highest total is declared the winner. In the case of two men totalling the same, the lighter man is the winner. There are weight classes in Olympic lifting just as there are in wrestling, judo, boxing, etc.

Q. What is meant by the term "spot reducing"? If it means being able to take weight off in certain areas I would like to try it. I have fat on my chin and stomach.

A. Yes, spot reducing does mean taking weight off in certain areas. For example, many women want to lose weight from their hips and thighs, but not from their face or bust areas. Now that you know what spot reducing is, you should also know that it works only with enormous effort. Sometimes fat may be chased away from an area by excessive activity, but this is not easily done. For example, a fat person who runs 10 miles a day may find that his legs are slightly more muscularly defined than his chest, which is not so involved in the activity. As a rule, however, exercise burns calories which help to unload fat from all over the body, rather than in any specialized area.

Many people feel that performing 20 or 30 sit-ups a night will reduce their stomachs. Nothing could be further from the truth. Sit-ups will firm and strengthen the abdominal muscles hidden beneath the pot belly, but the actual fat reduction is limited to an overall fat loss which is in direct proportion to the amount of energy (calories) burned up in the performance of the sit-ups (very few). A better activity for weight loss would be rope jumping, distance running, stair exercise or long walks. Here again, the excess weight removed is most efficiently lost by a reduction in overall calorie intake. The fat on your chin and stomach indicates that you are carrying excess weight all over. The ideal solution, of course, is a combination of toning exercises and reduced food intake.

INDEX